# Holy Trinity Church

# A Taste of History

**Edited by Ronnie Mulryne**

This book and its publication have been commissioned by the Friends of Shakespeare's Church. All proceeds go towards funding the conservation of Holy Trinity Church.

Publisher: Independent Publishing Network

Publication date: October 2019

ISBN: 978-1-78972-601-5


Distributor:   Friends of Shakespeare's Church

                Holy Trinity Church

                Old Town, Stratford-upon-Avon

                Warwickshire, CV37 6BG

                office@stratford-upon-avon.org


First Edition 2014  (ed. Ronnie Mulryne)

Second Edition 2019  (ed. Lindsay MacDonald)


Set in 12-point Times New Roman

Printed on a Ricoh c751ex colour production system by Printdomain, Rotherham

## Preface to the Second Edition

This revised and updated edition has been prepared in tribute to its editor and co-author, Dr Ronnie Mulryne, who passed away in January 2019.

He was Emeritus Professor of English and Comparative Literature at the University of Warwick, where he had been active for many years in the field. He inspired the inter-disciplinary study of European Renaissance culture and of the plays of Shakespeare and his contemporaries in performance.

In Stratford-upon-Avon, Ronnie's enthusiasm resulted in collaboration between scholars of history, education and performance studies, archivists and experts in architecture and restoration, to publish a study of the Guild and Guild Buildings of Shakespeare's Stratford. This, in turn, led him to work tirelessly to establish Shakespeare's Schoolroom and Guildhall as a major heritage destination. He was a Trustee of the Shakespeare Birthplace Trust, a Governor of the Royal Shakespeare Company, Chairman of Governors and Trustee of King Edward VI School, President of the Stratford Choral Society, and Chairman of the Friends of Shakespeare's Church. He was active in Holy Trinity Church as a warden, reader and communion server. He was also instrumental in the restoration of the Becket Chapel and the re-development of St Peter's Chapel.

Ronnie's energy, charm, generosity in encouraging others, and his love of theatre, music, poetry, architecture and history have been an inspiration to everyone who knew him. He is greatly missed.

Lindsay MacDonald (Editor)

*Watercolour of south elevation, early sketch proposal for extension*
*(Stephen Oliver, Architect).*

# Contents

*The Chancel of Holy Trinity Church.*

# 1

## Introduction and Acknowledgements

### Ronnie Mulryne

*Chairman of the Friends of Shakespeare's Church*

Holy Trinity is a Church that lives and worships in the present. There is a large and active congregation, as well as satellite groups and organisations – a modern worship group, numerous house groups, a church for young families in the grounds of a shopping centre, a food bank – which radiate out from the core of the Church's common life, expressed in daily acts of worship in the ancient church building. Yet, alongside this vigorous Christian life there exists an appetite for information about the building's eventful history, its conservation and restoration, and the lives of the people who have built and worshipped here across the centuries.

It was to respond to this interest that a series of talks named 'A Taste of History' was delivered in late 2013 in the church's superb Chancel. The Friends of Shakespeare's Church, who commissioned the talks, encouraged by the positive response of the large group of parishioners and others who attended – some 80 people on each occasion, sometimes more – decided to publish this booklet. The Friends also asked for the illustrated talk delivered at their AGM in May 2014, dealing with the historic Becket Chapel, to be included.

This book is concerned initially, though not exclusively, with the restoration and conservation of the Church's historic fabric, a prime responsibility of the Friends, who have raised more than £1m towards conservation since 2003. The well-being and beauty of the Church have to an extent been secured by these efforts. The clerestories have been repaired, the north transept has been refurbished and re-ordered, stained-glass windows have been restored and repairs have been undertaken to the

1

spire and the chancel roof. Most obviously, perhaps, the beautiful Clopton Chapel has been conserved, as have the historic monuments in the Chancel. Conservation has also been undertaken on the Shakespeare monument and the Shakespeare family gravestones. Much remains to be done. The Friends are drawing up plans for the conservation of the Becket chapel in the south aisle and St Peter's chapel in the south transept. Stonework needs constant attention, and we are already aware of problems that require both urgent and long-term treatment. We hope that this book may encourage readers to help us carry out our task of beautifying, restoring and conserving this wonderful building as a fitting place for worship and prayer.

*St Peter's Chapel in the South Transept,*
*following conservation and refurbishment in 2015.*

## The Book and its Contributors

Restoration and conservation, in addition to their primary functions, open the way to exploring the Church's rich history. Documentary and visual evidence has been called on in several chapters to support expert examination of the fabric. We are enormously grateful to our Church architect, Mr Stephen Oliver, author of one of the chapters in this book, who has led the conservation of the building over recent years. Stephen's chapter summarises in broad outline the history of his predecessors' work and celebrates the Church's great good fortune in attracting over the years the services of gifted architectural and stained-glass practitioners. His own contribution to our building will fittingly stand with theirs into the future.

We owe a great debt also to Mr David Odgers, whose outstanding skills as a conservator have brought to light many of the previously hidden beauties of the Clopton Chapel. He has also restored, as he discusses in his chapter, various Chancel monuments, several of them historically significant in their craftsmanship and in the light they throw on important figures in the Church's history. David's research also reveals the doubtful practices sometimes applied to these remarkable artefacts as a result of misguided attempts at 'restoration'. This is the case with the famous monument to William Shakespeare. As David reveals, the history of the monument's 'restoration' emerges as a patchwork of botched attempts at restoring a fancifully-conceived 'original', a process that went as far as whitewashing the monument to reproduce the supposed appearance of classical sculpture. We are fortunate that more recent work, and in particular David's supremely careful and sympathetic conservation, has restored the monument to a state that is as close to its original condition as modern materials and skilful expertise can achieve.

Mairi Macdonald's distinction as the editor of the authoritative and comprehensive published edition of the records of the Stratford Guilds, and her long experience as an archivist, are everywhere apparent in her original and fascinating study of the convergence and, from time to time, the growing apart of the town's two main religious foundations, the College, based at Holy Trinity, and the Guild, based in the town centre at the Guild Chapel. The Guild maintained chapels in Holy Trinity until the Reformation put paid to them – as it did to the Becket Chapel, the chief site of the College's public worship and the source of its wealth and prominence. Mairi shows that despite, or perhaps because of, the closeness and shared responsibilities between College and Guild, contention and rivalry were never far from the surface. She provides, moreover, a wealth of documentary evidence to give the reader a vivid sense of the pre-Reformation life of both Guild and College, their connections with the Church and the day-to-day affairs that drew them together and prised them apart.

*The Guild Almshouses (in the foreground), the Guildhall and the Guild Chapel.*

Dr Robert Bearman is Stratford's foremost local historian, as well as a Shakespearean interpreter of distinction and the editor of volumes of the indispensable *Minutes and Accounts of the Stratford-upon-Avon Corporation*. The first of his two chapters in this book provides a new account of the Shakespeare family gravestones, drawing on extensive research to show that, while uncertainties remain about the gravestones' recent and distant history, there is every scholarly reason to argue not only that Shakespeare was buried in Holy Trinity, but that his original gravestone remains in place and his grave unopened.

Bearman's second chapter explores the history of the Church's south transept, now St Peter's Chapel. It also studies the Church's south aisle. Each of these is of the greatest architectural and historic interest but each is little studied in previous publications. After a long and eventful architectural history, which Bearman outlines, St Peter's was re-dedicated as a memorial to those who fought in the First World War. The south aisle hosts the Becket Chapel, arguably the most historically rich of all the sites of worship in the ancient Church. We are more than grateful to Robert for sharing his extensive and meticulous scholarship with us, and his knowledge of Stratford's long history.

The events that led to the foundation of the Becket Chapel and the personalities involved in its early history are the subject of my own chapter. This traces the history lying behind what is now an undistinguished-looking place of worship. Few even among Sunday communicants at the Chapel are conscious of the extraordinary people and turbulent events which led to its pre-Reformation status as a symbol of fundamental tensions between Church and State. Fewer know that it was once an active and imposing centre of worship to which the people of Stratford flocked. Exceptionally, the Becket Chapel and its College of Priests became, legally speaking, the 'owner' of the Collegiate Church itself. We can count ourselves fortunate that, after the destruction of the

Chapel at the Reformation, a tangible recollection survives in the mensa or surface stone of Holy Trinity's High Altar, a stone that was once the capping stone of the altar raised in 1331 or shortly after to honour the martyred Thomas Becket.

*The Becket chapel as it is now.*

### Sources and Acknowledgements

The editor owes a great deal, not only to the contributors to this book but also to previous historians of Holy Trinity. The excellent *Shakespeare's Church: a Parish for the World* (2010), written and edited by Val Horsler, with Martin Gorick and Paul Edmundson, has been a constant source of reliable information. In 1902 or shortly after J. Harvey Bloom, Rector of Whitchurch, published *Shakespeare's Church, Otherwise the Collegiate Church of the Holy Trinity of Stratford-upon-Avon*, still valuable as an account by an insider of the Church and its history. Other historians and antiquarians, including William Dugdale, Robert Bell Wheler, John

Jordan and James Halliwell, provide vivid glimpses of the church as it evolved across the centuries. The invaluable archives of the Shakespeare Birthplace Trust, which hold many documents from Holy Trinity as well as abundant materials relating to the history of the town and its people, remain a source that frequently throws up new discoveries. I am grateful to Dr Diana Owen, the Trust's director, for permission to draw on these archives and to Madeleine Cox, one of the Trust's librarians. I am also grateful to John Cheal, recently a member of the Holy Trinity congregation and a former Head Verger, who has allowed us free use of his photographs of many aspects of the Church. The generosity of these and other photographers and copyright holders, including Susan Swann, King Edward Sixth School, David Odgers, Stephen Oliver, Richard Lithgow and William Mulryne, is acknowledged in relation to the individual photographs and/or permissions they supplied. I am grateful to Pat Pilton for his generous help with the layout of the book. Sincere thanks are also due to Mike Flowers, Deb Flowers and Antonia Lyon of Setsquare who have been most helpful and supportive advisors as well as master printers of the first edition of this book.

I should like to thank most warmly, Jonathan Drake, my collaborator throughout the lengthy and sometimes arduous process of bringing this book together. Jonathan's skills as a photographer and master of computer technology, and his rigorous editorial assistance, have been invaluable.

Finally, I acknowledge and thank the Trustees of the Friends of Shakespeare's Church who commissioned and encouraged this publication, the Wardens and Parochial Church Council of Holy Trinity who sanctioned it, and especially the Vicar and Associate Vicar, the Rev Patrick Taylor and the Rev Steve Bate, who have given us their full support. I also gladly thank the parishioners of Holy Trinity, many of whom attended the talks and who as a worshipping body remain the custodians and stewards of the Church's long-continuing history.

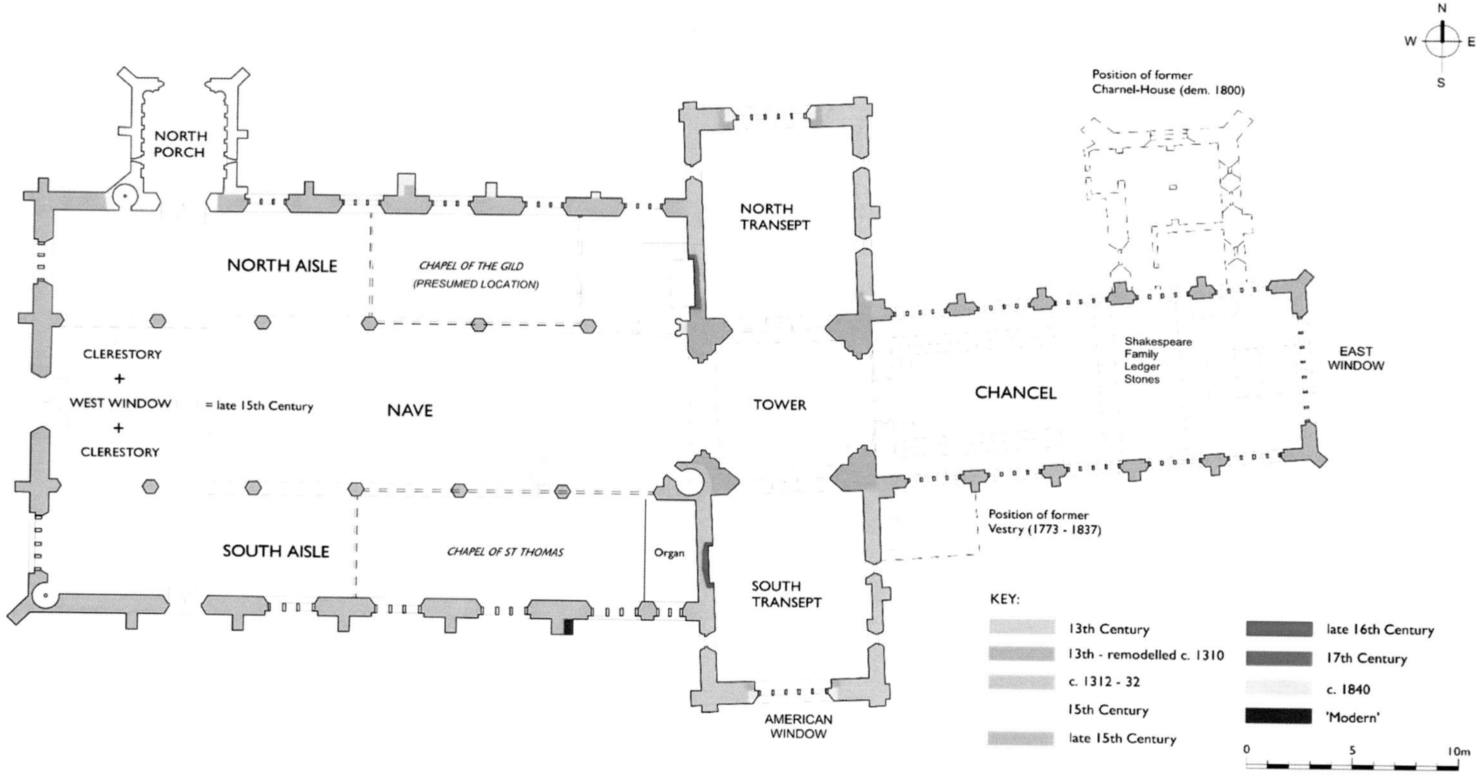

Position of former
Charnel-House (dem. 1800)

EAST
WINDOW

Shakespeare
Family
Ledger
Stones

CHANCEL

Position of former
Vestry (1773 - 1837)

NORTH
TRANSEPT

TOWER

SOUTH
TRANSEPT

AMERICAN
WINDOW

Organ

CHAPEL OF THE GILD
(PRESUMED LOCATION)

CHAPEL OF ST THOMAS

NAVE

NORTH AISLE

SOUTH AISLE

NORTH
PORCH

CLERESTORY

WEST WINDOW

CLERESTORY

= late 15th Century

N E
W S

0    5    10m

KEY:

13th Century

13th - remodelled c. 1310

c. 1312 - 32

15th Century

late 15th Century

late 16th Century

17th Century

c. 1840

'Modern'

# 2

## Conservation and Restoration of Holy Trinity Church

### Stephen Oliver

*Architect to Holy Trinity Church*

Holy Trinity Church is best known as the church in which William Shakespeare was baptised and in which he lies buried. It receives hundreds of thousands of visitors annually as a result. However, Shakespeare's life represents only 52 years within the more than 800 years of the building's history. It is appropriate, therefore, that this book should begin with a brief overview of the architecture of such a historic church, and outline, as a prelude to more detailed discussions to follow, some of the conservation and restoration projects undertaken over the years.

Perhaps it would be best, first of all, to summarise in a broad fashion the chronology of the building's development, as shown in the plan opposite. The oldest part of the present building, the north and south transepts, the crossing and the tower, date back to c.1210, although there are references to a place of worship being in existence much earlier. The nave and the north and south aisles date back to the 14th century, though the aisles have been considerably modified since that date, while the chancel, north porch, clerestories and west window were added in the 15th century. So, by the time Shakespeare was baptised in 1564, the general plan of the church building would have been much as it is today.

One of the key figures in the building's early history, and indeed in 14th century England, was John de Stratford. Born around 1275, probably in Stratford, to a prosperous and influential family, he was educated at Oxford, was a doctor of civil law and became Rector of Holy Trinity in 1317. He was Dean of the Court of Arches in the 1320s, accumulating ecclesiastical benefices such as the Archdeaconry of Lincoln. When the

*View of church from the east, across the river, in 1889.*

bishopric of Winchester fell vacant, he was chosen to deliver letters from Edward II to the Pope in favour of Robert Baldock's succession, but the Pope chose Stratford for the post instead, infuriating the king. John de Stratford later played a role in the deposition of Edward II and the accession of Edward III. He became Chancellor of England in 1330 and in 1331 founded a chantry chapel in Holy Trinity's south aisle. This chapel, used for the celebration of masses for the souls of donors, had its own priests housed in a building close by, known as the 'College'. Stratford became Archbishop of Canterbury in 1333, and is buried in Canterbury Cathedral. Holy Trinity is arguably one of the very few parish churches in England where John de Stratford's historical significance could be overshadowed by the fame of a later church member.

Before we look at some of the projects that have been undertaken in the church, it is helpful to consider the terms 'restoration' and 'conservation' in a little more detail. While the two words are often used almost interchangeably, the difference is perhaps best illustrated by the debate among architects and other interested parties in the 19th century. Many Victorian architects favoured 'restoration', which was often highly destructive. This approach was challenged by the art critic John Ruskin in his *Seven Lamps of Architecture*, published in 1849. Ruskin wrote, "Take proper care of your monuments, and you will not need to restore them". The Society for the Protection of Ancient Buildings (SPAB) was founded by William Morris in 1877, to counteract the extreme so-called 'restoration' of medieval buildings. A letter of 1881 indicates, in fact, that the Society, as an actively campaigning organization, took an interest in proposed work to Holy Trinity Church.

A review of the archival records shows that Holy Trinity has attracted the interest and involvement, not only of campaigning theorists, but also of a number of prominent craftsmen, both local and national. *The Literary World* published an engraving in 1839 deriving from a fine drawing by

*Butterfield's engraving of the Chancel after the restoration of 1835.*

William Butterfield and incorporating details from the architect Harvey Eginton. Butterfield was assistant to Eginton, who was based in Worcester and carried out a great deal of work at Holy Trinity, including the new chancel roof in 1835. Butterfield set up his own architectural practice in London in 1840, and his long list of achievements includes designing Keble College in Oxford as well as many churches.

George Bodley and Thomas Garner were among the leading ecclesiastical architects of the late 19th Century. They were responsible in 1899 for designing the organ case installed in the nave above the crossing and still in place today. However, even such prominent architects did not escape scrutiny: *The Times* published a letter from William Morris in 1890, setting out his opposition to some of their intended work for Holy Trinity.

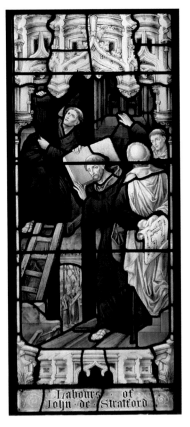

*The labours of John de Stratford overseeing building of the Becket chapel, depicted in the south window of St Peter's chapel.*

Holy Trinity is fortunate to have such superb windows, which represent the cumulative efforts of a number of skilled craftsmen over the centuries. Although we have no record of the stonemason responsible for the stonework around the chancel and clerestory windows, the similarities with the architecture of Stratford's Guild Chapel suggest that it may well have been Thomas Dowland, who worked on a number of churches in Warwickshire and Worcestershire in the late 15th Century.

*The east window, produced by Heaton, Butler & Bayne, installed in 1894.*

William Holland & Co of Warwick was commissioned to supply glass for the church's new east window in 1850. However, all seven lights were not filled until 1859, as and when funds became available. Holland exhibited many panels of his work at the 1851 Great Exhibition; it is highly likely that some of the panels for Holy Trinity's east window were there. The Holland glass was removed in 1894 to make way for glass produced by Heaton, Butler & Bayne, one of the major late 19th Century stained-glass firms. This London-based firm, founded in 1855 by Clement Heaton (who had previously worked for Holland), continued in production after Heaton's death in 1882. Fashions

*A detail from the 'Hidden Window' formerly in the Becket Chapel.*

were changing, and Holland's preferred use of very strong colours and tortured scenes from Christ's Passion had fallen out of favour. Heaton & Co's window would nonetheless have been anathema to the church architect George Bodley, who preferred accurately-copied designs inspired by medieval practice. The story of William Holland's work for the great east window doesn't end in 1894. Four of his panels were re-used in a window that was once part of the Becket Chapel, but had to be boarded up in 1898, in order to accommodate pipework for the newly installed organ. This window was rediscovered when the organ was serviced in 2011, and in 2013 the glass was removed for conservation. The 'hidden window' has been infilled with plain leaded glass, and, following conservation, the Holland window has become a prominent feature of the recent extension to the south side of the church.

There are many less obvious evidences of the building's long history. For example, parishioners and visitors may notice some small, square holes in the wall of the south aisle. These are known as 'putlog' holes, and would have been used to support medieval scaffolding in the 1330s. There are also a number of examples of masons' marks (a mason's way of identifying his work), such as those on the stonework of the west window in the south transept.

As we have seen, the high profile of Holy Trinity Church has created challenges for church architects over the years, but there are also several benefits. The availability of historical drawings can help to shape decisions on current conservation projects. For example, the design for the south aisle pinnacles was based on an image from 1926 contained in the archive records. Equally, conservation can help with the documentation of the building's history. When recent conservation work

*Example of a 'putlog' hole in the masonry, observed with the aid of scaffolding.*

required the use of a high-level access platform, it also provided an opportunity to photograph details of the clerestory windows and organ casing that could not have been obtained from ground level. In addition, the most recent architectural drawings of the church were prepared in support of the south side extension.

We are very fortunate to benefit from the wonderful craftsmanship and long history that is so evident throughout the church. In return, we accept our responsibility to conserve the building for future generations, and to enhance the rich catalogue of images documenting its history.

## Addendum for Second Edition

Since the first edition of *A Taste for History* was published, a new chapter has been written in the long story of the architectural development of Holy Trinity Church. After many years of hard work, a new extension on the south side of the South Aisle was commenced in July 2015, being completed only just before the 400th anniversary of Shakespeare's death in April 2016. As the first extension to this Grade I listed church since the Reformation (apart from a

*View of new extension on south side.*

small Vestry south of the Chancel, built 1773, demolished 1837), there was a great deal of interest in its design. The new building provides a Vestry, WCs and storage, together with a suitable location to display the 1850 Holland glass salvaged from behind the organ. It seemed impossible to consider building in anything other than stone for such a setting, particularly where a stained glass window had to be reset, so the building has a consciously Gothic feel. It has local Cotswold stone walls, both rubblestone and dressings, with a stainless steel roof. The relocated window provides a focus for a new gabled porch, projecting from the existing south doorway. Our presentation drawings for early schemes, in watercolour, caught the imagination of the relevant authorities and so the path to gaining approval was much smoother than it might have been. Integral to the project was an archaeological excavation during which 304 burials of medieval to post-medieval date were lifted and documented.

*St. Peter's Chapel recreated in the South Transept.*

18

The scheme also included the complete reorganisation of the South Transept, recreating St Peter's Chapel by returning the screen to its earlier location, and allowing the war memorial to be seen. The space was refurnished (with Tibor Reich fabric, selected by the late Ronne Mulryne) and relit. Midland Conservation Ltd of Walsall were the contractors for this project and we were all delighted when it won several awards.

Several other projects have been undertaken. The new kitchenette at the west end of the South Aisle is a remarkably complex piece of joinery, which folds away to look like a piece of furniture, but opens out to provide a servery for tea and coffee after the service, as well as refreshments to visitors. The exterior of the South Transept has been repaired, with a considerable amount of new stone, including a newly carved apex cross.

*Apex cross on the South Transept gable.*

Planning for future phases continues, with the North Transept and the Bier House now the main priorities. The building remains in fine condition, owing to careful work over many centuries, and we must continue this important mission.

19

*The Shakespeare monument on the north wall of the Chancel.*

# 3

## Conservation of the Chancel Monuments

### David Odgers

*Conservator and Consultant*

*Leader of the team responsible for conservation works*

Following on from Stephen Oliver's overview of the church building's architecture and history I shall focus on the monuments in the chancel. Although this represents only a small part of the building, the work covers four centuries of monument design from the tomb of Dean Thomas Balsall, dated 1491, to the memorial to the Revd James Davenport of 1841. As we shall see, all the monuments have been amended over time, often in line with the fashion of a particular period. The chest tomb of Dean Thomas Balsall is positioned on the left hand side of the altar as you look into the chancel, just behind the Shakespeare family gravestones.

*The Balsall Tomb in the Chancel (1491).*

21

Thomas Balsall was Dean of the college and vicar of the church from 1466 until his death in 1491. The tomb is made of Cotswold stone, which was originally covered with a layer of white lead and then painted. The tomb was subsequently painted over white in the 1950s, but cross-section analysis of very fine fragments reveals yellow and red colours below this layer. The analysis also found traces of original gilding on the tomb. We have tried to remove as much as possible of what is now a grey layer of paint, using cotton wool swabs with acetone, and stopping as soon as any colour was encountered.

*The Balsall Tomb undergoing conservation.*

There is a recess on top of the tomb, which suggests that there would have been a brass figure placed there originally. We have also made use of archive records to inform our work, and were interested to find a photograph from the 1890s showing a block of stone which appears to be weighting down the lid. The iron within the chest structure had started to corrode, which had caused the top to lift. This was rectified during the conservation work by replacing the corroded iron with stainless steel.

Moving slightly further from the altar, we come to the most famous items in the chancel: the Shakespeare monument, and the Shakespeare family gravestones. As Robert Bearman discusses these in more detail later in this book, I will confine myself to the monument itself and the works that have been undertaken on it over the years. The Shakespeare monument was attributed by William Dugdale to the sculptor Gerard Johnson (also known as Gheerart Janssen) in a diary entry dated 1645, and also by two other sources dated 1627. All three sources also attribute the tomb of John Combe to Johnson. Confusingly, perhaps, Johnson's father was also a sculptor by the same name, who had come to England from Holland and set up in London.

There are numerous images of the Shakespeare monument in the archives and, while it has been fairly well looked after, there have been some quite significant changes over the years. For example, one image from the late 19th Century shows the font bowl on the floor beneath the monument, while the window behind the monument was blocked up and the location of the steps was different. Some of the 'restorations' and repaintings are recorded in the church records, kept in the Shakespeare Birthplace Trust archive. An entry in the records mentions a reference in Wheler's *History and Antiquities* to the

*The Shakespeare bust, showing cleaning in progress.*

monument being 'carefully repaired and the original colours ... preserved [by Mr John Hall, a limner of Stratford] in 1748'. In 1793, however, 'meddling Malone' consented to 'daub it with white paint ... to suit the taste of the present age'. A later entry, dated March 1861, records members of the Birthplace committee '... assembled in the chancel ... to witness the effect of the restoration of the bust of Shakespeare to its original colours'. This 1861 restoration was carried out by a Mr Collins who is recorded as having removed the white paint and 'touch(ed) with colour several defective places … [but] rigidly preserve(d) the ancient tones'. The columns of black marble are also recorded as having been repaired at this time by a Mr Vincent, a Stratford-on-Avon sculptor. We also learn that 'much defacement has been perpetrated by some senseless nonentities scratching their insignificant names on the marble tablets'. The two cherubs above the monument represent Labour and Rest and it appears on inspection that their reverse sides were never painted.

Research showed that the white paint was indeed partly cleaned off the Shakespeare bust during the nineteenth century restoration, as detailed in the archives, although it was not removed from the face and hands, and only partially from the coat. The coat was then repainted, as were the red sleeves, the hair, the cushion and the background to the figure. Our restoration report also refers to finding a varnish layer in almost all of the cross-sections taken, which is thought to date from sometime between the late nineteenth and the early twentieth century.

Evidence of a post-World War II restoration was also found. In this restoration the face and cushion were retouched, but other areas such as the hands, collar, cuffs and parts of the coat were completely repainted. The paint used contained titanium white which dates the re-paint probably to sometime after the 1950s. As part of the same scheme a brown glaze appears to have been brushed over the surface and partly wiped off, to imitate the effect of a discoloured brown varnish. Re-gilding of all the gold areas using a bright yellow size, tinted with chromed yellow, is thought to date from the same restoration. The problem with the brown glaze is that it gets darker over time. It is very difficult to remove such varnish without also removing the paint underneath and so, as the fashion today is not to interfere with the monument, the glaze was not removed during the recent conservation. However, the whole monument was carefully cleaned.

*The Tomb of John Combe in the Chancel (1614).*

The monument to John Combe, dated 1614, is also attributed to Gerard Johnson and is positioned behind the high altar on the left hand side as you look into the chancel. John Combe was a friend of Shakespeare and left money to the church and to the town. The conservation work has made a significant difference to the background of this monument, which had been regularly coated with beeswax that had subsequently discoloured. This was successfully removed by using microporous sponges and a mixture of water and white spirit with some warming. The removal of the wax has also helped to clarify the wording of the inscription.

*The Monument to James Kendall (1751).*

The monument to James Kendall, dated 1751, has benefited significantly from the removal of dirt from the pores of the marble (left).

Similarly, the cleaning of the wall-mounted memorial of Revd James Davenport (d.1841) has had a dramatic effect, both for the rendering of detail in the stonework and the legibility of the text against the white marble background.

*Rev James Davenport memorial on the north wall of the chancel.*

*Cleaning the angel at the apex of the Davenport memorial, using a 'dry-steam' cleaner, which emits a jet of steam at 160°C.*

27

On the north wall of the chancel in front of the eastern-most window, almost above the Balsall tomb, is the poignant monument to Richard and Judith Combe, who were cousins and betrothed to be married. The inscription records the sad fact that: 'she tooke her last leave of this life ... in ye arms of him, who most entirely loved and was beloved of her even to ye very death'. Cleaning of the marble has greatly enhanced the appearance of the two figures.

*The Monument to Richard and Judith Combe (1649)*

Finally, on the south wall of the chancel, the memorial to Elizabeth Rawlins (d.1869) showed considerable evidence of previous repair, particularly on the pilasters. There was some disruption at cornice and capital level where joints were opening. The surface was slightly dirty and about 40% of the filling in the inscriptions was missing. Investigation revealed that the top of the monument was loose because of the corrosion of rusting iron fixings. Further investigation revealed that the support for the upper part of the monument was an iron bar decorated with a *fleur de lys*. Could this have been an old piece of railing that was re-purposed?

*The fleur de lys support found incorporated in the Rawlings memorial, after treatment to inhibit rust.*

The inscription on the monument was originally produced by cutting the letters into the slate background and then filling them. However, over time, some of this filling had fallen away making the inscription difficult to read. This has been addressed by re-filling the lettering.

*Filling the incised letters with a lime-based filler, which was then toned in with acrylic paints.*

I hope that this brief review will give readers an insight not only into the conservation process, but also into the wealth of history incorporated within the chancel monuments, in addition to the remarkable memorial of its most famous occupant.

*The Shakespeare Family Gravestones in the Chancel.*

# 4

## The Shakespeare Family Ledger Stones and What They Tell Us

### Robert Bearman

*Former Head of Archives and Local Studies, Shakespeare Birthplace Trust, and author of studies of Stratford buildings and local history*

The epitaph on Shakespeare's monument records his death on 23 April 1616 and, on the evidence of the parish register, he was buried three days later, on 26 April. That is about as far as we can get with what we might call material evidence. In his will, Shakespeare made no specific provision for a place of burial, or for the placing of a memorial, simply committing 'my bodye to the Earth whereof yt ys made'. He could, like Roger Sadler, who died in 1578, have asked for burial 'at my seates end'; or like Peter Smart, who died in 1588, 'nighe the seate where I did accustomablie use to sitt' or even, like Margaret Reynolds, who died in 1615, in the chancel. If he had been keen to leave an even greater mark, he could, like John Combe, who died in 1615, have left £60 for the erection of a tomb chest in the chancel, 'near unto my mother's grave'. But, unluckily for those wishing to prove he was buried in the church, he left no such instructions, only this humble request to return his body to the earth.

However, given that Shakespeare's name does not, in fact, appear on the gravestone generally accepted as his, how sure can we be that he was buried there? William Dugdale, in his *Antiquities of Warwickshire*, published in 1656, states without any doubt that near Shakespeare's monument on the north wall of the chancel: 'lyeth a plaine free stone underneath which his body is buried with this Epitaph, Good freind for Iesus sake forbeare ...' etc. We also have good evidence that Dugdale saw this 'stone' some twenty years earlier, in the mid-1630s, when he copied the inscription. On top of that, John Weever, who died in 1632, clearly assumed, in an undated note, an identical place of burial, recording the same verse 'vpo[n] the grave stone' of 'William Shakespeare the famous poet'. So, within eighteen years of Shakespeare's death, and doubtless well before, we know for certain that this stone was being pointed out as

*The Gravestone of William Shakespeare, showing damage.*

his. To all intents and purposes, the wording on the gravestone reads the same today as it did when Dugdale transcribed it, so there is no real mileage in the idea that only part of the stone survives today and that on some missing part there was once a more formal account of whose stone we are looking at. Whether or not the stone was re-cut or even replaced will be discussed later, but on the basic point of whether this wording is authentic, and that that is all there ever was, the evidence is clear.

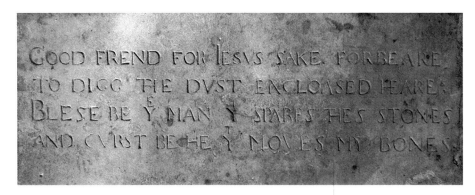

*The malediction on Shakespeare's Gravestone.*

Some have suggested that Shakespeare himself composed the wording but this is far less certain. Sir Francis Fane, quoting only the last two lines in the mid-1650s, attributed them to Shakespeare, and in 1693 John Dowdall declared, on the assurance of the parish clerk, that the entire inscription was 'made by himselfe'. The following year, William Hall claimed that Shakespeare ordered the epitaph 'to be cut upon his tomb-stone', adding that he was buried 'seventeen foot deep'. However, if Shakespeare had feared disinterment, as the malediction makes clear, then the easiest way of avoiding this would have been to request burial in the church – which, at least on the evidence of his will, he didn't.

Alongside the complete absence of Shakespeare's name from his gravestone, another problem arises when we come to consider Shakespeare's monument on the north wall of the chancel, attributed to Gheerart Janssen the younger. On the evidence of a dedicatory poem included in the First Folio of 1623, with its reference to 'thy Stratford Moniment', we can assume it must have been put up by that date. But the wording on the monument is curious, firstly, and remarkably, in not giving Shakespeare's baptismal (and therefore his Christian) name. The wording is also misleading, if not absurd, in its statement that 'Death hath plast, with in this monument Shakespeare', clearly not the case. Diana Price has

33

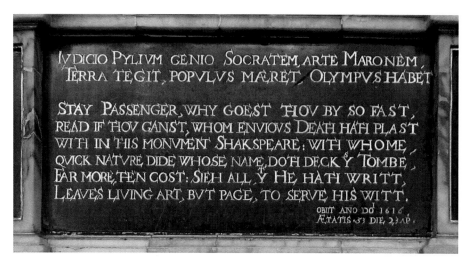

*Wording on the Shakespeare monument.*

come up with a persuasive explanation for these oddities, namely that the monument was not commissioned by Shakespeare's family but by his professional colleagues, members of the King's Men, who had easy access to sculptor Janssen's workshop in Southwark, and had assumed that the monument would be placed over a tomb chest on which Shakespeare's name would be conventionally recorded. Many examples of this sort of arrangement survive, and it may indeed have been the case that his family simply chose not to mark his grave in a conventional way or, rather, perhaps misunderstood what was being planned in London, and then didn't have the means, or the inclination, to remedy the situation by erecting such an expensive memorial as a tomb chest. The result was that only the bust, paid for by Shakespeare's colleagues, was erected.

Has the stone always been in its present position or was it re-laid, along with the other family stones, to make an impressive row? We know from illustrations made by William Thomas for his revised edition of Dugdale's *Warwickshire*, published in 1730, and by John Jordan, Thomas Walford and R.B. Wheler, that by the end of the eighteenth century the chancel and

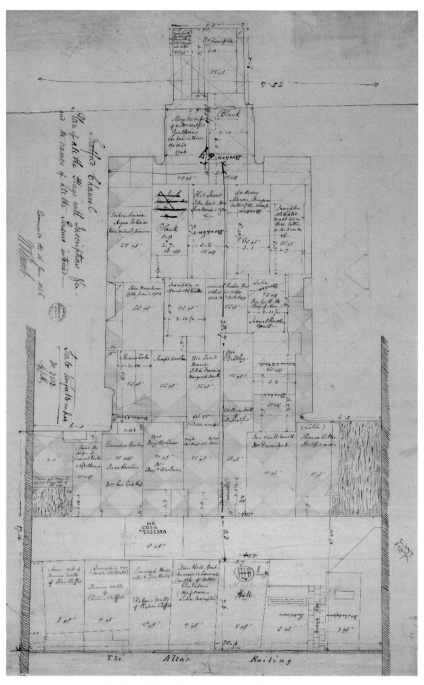

*Measured plan of the Chancel (1836) showing gravestones.*
*The 'Shakespeare Stones', numbered 1 to 5, are shown running along the bottom.*

sanctuary floors were largely made up of ledger stones. So when in 1836, a measured plan was drawn up prior to restoration of the main chancel, the floor is indeed shown as almost completely covered with such stones, and with Shakespeare's and his family's stones firmly in their present positions. So moving the Shakespeare stones for the benefit of visitors to the town (which would surely not have happened until well into the eighteenth century) would have been altogether too complicated a process. In any case, we also have a drawing by George Vertue of 1737 which shows quite clearly that Shakespeare's tomb was roughly in the same position as shown in the 1836 plan, as indeed was his wife Anne's.

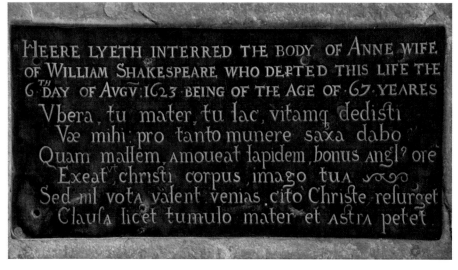

*Inscription on the gravestone of Anne Shakespeare, d.1623.*

Anne Shakespeare died on 6 August 1623 and was buried two days later. Her grave is marked by the brass plate fixed to a stone close adjoining Shakespeare's to the north. This is its position as recorded by George Vertue in 1737 showing that its wording corresponds to Dugdale's transcription made at least by 1656 and perhaps by 1634.

The remaining family stones raise intriguing questions. From north to south, first recorded by Dugdale by 1656, we have Thomas Nash, who died in 1647, the first husband of Shakespeare's grand-daughter Elizabeth Hall. Then John Hall, Elizabeth's father, who died in 1635, the husband of Shakespeare's daughter Susanna, and finally Susanna Hall herself, who died in 1649. We know from later sources that they were re-cut (see below) but they still clearly represent the wording that was originally inscribed on them.

*The gravestone of Thomas Nash, d.1647.*

However, there are problems. Firstly, they are not in a chronological sequence – we might have expected 1635 (John Hall), 1647 (Nash) and 1649 (Susanna) but instead we have 1647, 1635 and 1649. It could be that on Hall's death in 1635, a space had been left between his stone and Shakespeare's, so that Susanna could be buried between her father and her husband but that, on Nash's premature death in 1647, but before Susanna's in 1649, there had been a change of plan. There is a further oddity. The last two lines of John Hall's epitaph: *'Ne tumulo quid desit adest fidissima conjux / Et vitae Comitem nunc quoque mortis habet'*, may be translated: 'So that nothing should be lacking to his tomb, his most faithful wife is here / And the companion of his life is now also with him in death'. These lines couldn't have been composed before Susanna's death in 1649 as recorded on her stone, fourteen years after Hall's. So were these two lines added on or soon after Susanna's death (though in time for Dugdale to have recorded them by 1656)?

*The gravestone of John Hall, d.1635.*

I don't find this very convincing. Both John's and Susanna's inscriptions start off in very similar form (HEERE LYETH YE BODY OF ...) and with the same idiosyncratic spelling. Perhaps Nash's death in 1647 had sparked off a new and more elaborate way of commemorating the family. Nash was a man of real wealth (unlike Hall) and might well have left enough to have paid for this. His inscription doesn't start quite the same (HEERE RESTETH YE BODY OF ...) but HEERE is spelt in the same fashion and the style of the lettering is the same. So perhaps his stone therefore came first, to be followed by a retrospective one for Hall, done at the same time as Susanna's two years later in order to explain that awkward couplet on Hall's saying that they were now joined in death. This wouldn't necessarily mean that Hall wasn't buried there, only that a grander series of stones, initiated on Nash's burial, led to John Hall's more elaborate commemoration. And there is another possibility: a month before Susanna's death, her widowed daughter Elizabeth had married as her second husband the well-to-do John Bernard. Perhaps it was he who came up with the money to commemorate the family. But amidst all this uncertainty, what we can be sure about is that all this was done by 1656 when Dugdale first recorded the inscriptions.

There is a further issue with Susanna Shakespeare's ledger stone. In September 1691 a grave seems to have been dug to its immediate south for the burial of Francis Watts of Ryon Clifford. Then his wife Ann, who died in 1704, was buried next to him, in the last vacant space further to the south. But when three years later, in 1707, Richard Watts, probably Francis's brother, died, there was a problem. With no room for a further ledger stone to the south, the famous epitaph on the lower part of Susanna Shakespeare's ledger stone, beginning 'Witty above her sex', was somehow scrubbed off and Watts's details recorded in its place. In the 1790s Vicar Davenport

*The gravestone of Susanna Hall (née Shakespeare) d.1649, showing the badly-damaged inscription.*

copied the inscriptions with a line drawn between them, even going so far as to say that there were two stones; 'For the stone has been cut asunder in the middle where I have drawn my line ... and another half stone joined to it.' Was Susanna Shakespeare's stone, covering an individual burial chamber, actually lifted and Watts's body inserted? Or was one of the adjoining Watts ledger stones lifted and the body inserted there but, because there was insufficient space on the stone, his inscription was simply somehow superimposed on Susanna's adjoining one instead?

*Sketch of Shakespeare's monument from the notebook of George Vertue, made when visiting Stratford with the Earl of Oxford in 1737.*

The next event of significance in the story of Susanna's stone was the visit to Stratford of the Reverend William Harness in 1844. He obligingly kept a diary of his visit, recording, amongst other things, that on 5 September the vicar, John Clayton, 'Walked with us to the Church and consented to my restoring the inscription on Mrs Hall's tombstone' to include the lines obliterated on the burial of Richard Watts. On the following day he went 'to the church to see the man progressing with the restoration of Mrs Hall's epitaph'. On 12 September, buoyed up with his success, he 'called on Mr Clayton with the purpose of speaking to him about restoring the inscriptions on all the Shakespearian tomb stones .. he gave me his consent to do all I wished and orders were immediately given for the same'. He followed this up with three later visits to inspect the work, the last on 19 September, the day of his departure, when he 'had a long talk with the man who is cutting the Shakespearian tombstones'. Finally, on 24 October, he wrote to R.B. Wheler, the Stratford antiquarian: 'I have to return you many thanks for your kind assistance in seeing that the mason did his work in an artistlike manner on the Shakespeare gravestones. Kite [the parish clerk] tells me that things are restored quite to your satisfaction. I trust this is the case for then I should be satisfied the inscriptions are exactly as they ought to be'.

*Engraving of chancel in 1824. Note ledger stones running to edge of step, and wooden altar rail, plaster ceiling, and masonry behind Shakespeare monument.*

Expert and thorough examination of the stones might yet reveal the true extent of this re-cutting, or, of course, if no re-cutting shows up, whether the stones themselves were actually replaced. But the big question is whether they cover individual burial chambers, a family vault, burials directly in the earth, or even no burials at all in those particular locations. We do know, from the evidence of later restoration work, that numerous vaults and burial chambers were discovered, especially in the chancel, south transept and the south aisle, and burials in the earth in the less prestigious north aisle and north transept. So, on the face of it, stones marking places of burial, are likely to be generally reliable. But, as far as the later Shakespeare stones are concerned, some overhaul might have occurred after Susanna Hall's death; and we do at least know for certain that they were re-cut in the 1840s.

41

TOMB OF SHAKESPERE IN THE CHANCEL OF THE HOLY TRINITY CHURCH, STRATFORD.

*Layout of the ledger stones in 1847.*

In summary, there may be no exactly contemporary material evidence to prove that William Shakespeare was buried beneath the maledictory stone, but the circumstantial evidence from as early as the 1630s is very strong, certainly sufficient to make it very likely. The wording on the ledger stones is substantially that recorded by Dugdale in 1656 and there is thus no reason to doubt its essential integrity, though we know that three of the stones at least (Thomas Nash's, John Hall's and Susanna Hall's) were re-cut in the 1840s and that, in the case of Susanna Hall's, this also included the complete re-instatement of the epitaph which had been erased in the early eighteenth century.

There were several occasions during the nineteenth century, particularly in the mid-1830s and in the 1890s, when alterations in the chancel affected the setting of the ledger stones, even though they were not moved. The ground plan of the chancel floor, prepared in 1836, including the Shakespeare family ledger stones, shows that, apart from the whole chancel floor being made up of ledger stones:

- at its east end was a step, 3ft 3ins wide, incorporated into which was a single ledger stone;
- this was followed by a second step some 7ft 6ins deep, taken up almost exclusively by the row of Shakespeare ledger stones;
- these ledger stones generally ran to the very western edge of this step as confirmed by early drawings/engravings;
- this second step, at its very northern end appears angled out westward at around 45°. This angled step is shown in Vertue's drawing of 1737 and in another of a hundred years later. Presumably it was to facilitate passage through the door to the charnel house (demolished in 1800).

The underlying objective of the restoration committee, formed in 1835, was to improve the overall condition of the chancel in recognition of its importance as the last resting place of Shakespeare and his family. This involved the laying of a new floor in the main part of the chancel. In the process, the old ledger stones were covered over or removed but not before the 1836 measured plan was drawn up, including notes of those inscriptions which could still be read.

Two important decisions were then made:

1.  the second (middle) step was brought forward and a row of stones inserted between its new edge and the 'Shakespeare' ledger stones. Subsequent photographs and engravings show a shallower first step with the edge of the second step no longer formed by the Shakespeare stones. The effect was to 'square off' the angled step referred to above;

2.  more surprisingly, the third (top) step was also brought forward, reducing the visible length of the Shakespeare ledger stones, from around 7ft 6ins shown in the measured plan of 1836 to the c.5ft 6ins which we see today. At its south end this step was angled out at 90°, partially obscuring Ann Watts's ledger stone, as if to create a platform below the *sedilia*.

Whether the stones were, or were not, lifted or disturbed in this process is not clear. The 1836 plan shows three rows of 'Norman' tiles between the Shakespeare stone and Anne Shakespeare's. These are no longer there. More intriguing is a letter from John Poynder, lawyer and evangelist, to R.B. Wheler, dated 20 August 1841, in which he comments: 'I can only live in hope that by some unfortunate slip of the spade where the brick wall does not interpose, something or other may yet come to light, in spite of the terrible denunciation of the oft-quoted cautionary lines .... . Relying on your at least keeping a sharp look out, I beg you to believe ... John Poynder'. This certainly implies at least some physical movement of the stones in the vicinity. Today they do all look remarkably neat.

The second of the major 19th-century restorations reached the chancel in 1890. As far as the Shakespeare ledger stones were concerned, this involved a further remodelling of the steps, when it was decided to install a new heating system. The second (middle) step, renewed in marble, was brought forward, though this has been obscured by a later alteration whilst the third (top) step, including the projection at its south end, was also renewed in marble. The new heating system required the digging of trenches up against the east wall during which further discoveries were made. This included the ledger stone marking the burial place of Judith Combe which was 'raised and re-laid on the level of the new floor, thirteen inches from the north wall and as near as possible to its original position', where it can still be seen. However, the workmen weren't always so careful. One builder's account includes: 'Cutting away for heating pipes, building

*Inscription on the gravestone (ledger stone) of Judith Combe, including affectionate reference to her relationship with her husband-to-be.*

trenches and making good ... filling up vault and extra labour making good tile paving after removal of ledgers'. Such cavalier behaviour does make one wonder what might have happened elsewhere at other times. To his credit, this was all too much for Charles Flower who resigned from the restoration committee, complaining that 'on visiting the Church on Saturday [I] was shocked to see what was going on'. Finally, in 2009, the second ('middle') step was again brought forward, and the first step narrowed to its present width, on installation of a revised heating system.

We must now address the question of whether Shakespeare's tomb has ever been opened, accidentally or otherwise. The first hint that it might have been was based on something that happened in 1796, though nothing was put down in writing about it for twenty years. The vicar's wife, Margaret, was buried on 2 July 1796 in a vault beneath the chancel floor. Its position is clearly shown on the measured plan of 1836, not all that far from the Shakespeare stones. In 1815, Washington Irving was told by the sexton: 'a few years since, as some labourers were digging to make an adjoining vault, the earth caved in, so as to leave a vacant space almost like an arch, through which one might have reached into his grave. No one, however, presumed to meddle with his remains, so awfully guarded by a malediction; and lest any of the idle curious, or any collector of relics, should be tempted to commit depredations, the old sexton kept watch over the place for two days until the vault was finished. He told me that he had made bold to look in at the hole but could see neither coffin nor bones; nothing but dust'.

A variant version of the story was recorded by Nathan Drake in 1818: 'Notwithstanding the anathema pronounced by the bard on any disturbers of his bones, the churchwardens were so negligent a few years ago in digging the adjoining grave of Dr [sic] Davenport, to break a large cavity into the tomb of Shakspeare! Mr ... told the writer that he was excited by curiosity to push his head and shoulders through the cavity, that he saw the remains of the bard, and that he could easily have brought away his skull, but was deterred by the curse which the poet invoked on any of those who disturbed his remains'. However, as the 1836 plan reveals, the Davenport vault was at least 3ft 3ins west of any possible 'Shakespeare' vault. If any wall did fall in, allowing a view into a neighbouring chamber it would have been more likely to have been one of those on the north or south, rather than the east.

Much later, a similar tale resurfaced. In 1884, James Hare wrote to the Birmingham Weekly Post, recalling a visit to the church back in '1826 or

1827'. He said that he had then found an adjoining vault open which he and a few friends had been able to get into, from which they had a view into Shakespeare's vault but with nothing very exciting to be seen 'only a slight elevation of mouldering dust'. Can we believe this? The Davenport vault, dug in 1796, was opened in 1811 and 1821 to bury Margaret Davenport's children, and in 1841 for Davenport himself. But these dates don't match Hare's story, nor is there any evidence that any of the old stones, let alone those anywhere near Shakespeare's, recorded burials as late as 1827. The account was therefore probably a mischievous invention at a time when feelings were running high during an official campaign to open the grave.

In 1879, against this background, there was published an even more startling story that the tomb had been opened in 1794 and the skull removed, re-published five years later in pamphlet form together with an account that the skull had been re-discovered in a burial vault in Beoley church. The author, since identified as C.L. Langston, turns out to have been the then-current incumbent at Beoley, so the story, though made superficially credible through the clever use of circumstantial details, can in none of its essentials be confirmed, and is now generally regarded as witty satire.

However, we do need to consider more carefully a claim by J.O. Halliwell that the Shakespeare stone had actually been replaced. In 1881, Halliwell, in the first edition of his *Outlines of the Life of William Shakespeare*, declared that the Shakespeare ledger stone: 'had, by the middle of the last century, sunk below the level of the floor, and about fifty years ago had become so much decayed as to suggest a vandalic order for its removal, and, in its stead, to place a new slab, one which marks certainly the locality of the farewell lines, but indicates nothing more. The original memorial has wandered from its allotted station no one can tell whither'. In 1883, when the proposal to open the tomb became public, Halliwell wrote to the *Stratford Herald* and changed this to: 'The slab which now covers his grave is a new one belonging to the present century but it is believed that the original was left under the present one.' But this claim, together with the original statement that this had happened 'about fifty years ago' was challenged by Thomas Keyt, parish clerk since 1829, who insisted that the re-cutting exercise of the 1840s (see above) did not extend to the Shakespeare stone. Instead: 'At that time the dirt which had accumulated in the letters on Shakespeare's grave stone – and become hard – was carefully removed, which gave them a fresh appearance', provoking Halliwell to write to *The Times* defending in general

*Drawing of the ledger stones in 1890.*

terms his original claim that the stone had badly deteriorated but admitting 'that I may have been too precipitate in assuming that the transformation was effected so recently as 1835, the period at which the church was restored'. As a result, his 'fifty years ago' claim in the early editions of his *Outlines of the Life of William Shakespeare*, was changed in later ones to 'about ninety years ago'. Finally, in the course of a long letter to *The Times*, published on 30 January 1888, criticising all the recent restoration work, he again added that the original ledger stone had been 'replaced by another purchased from the yard of a modern stone-mason'.

Halliwell is normally a reliable witness, but in this instance his statements do need to be treated with some caution. It was in 1883, after a dispute with the Stratford Corporation, that he turned his back on the town for which he had done so much. Moreover, his last letter to *The Times*, written a year before his death, reveals a long-standing unhappiness about the restoration of the parish church. So the fact that he was obliged to modify his initial claim twice does make it suspect, especially as he had fallen out with the Stratford dignitaries by that time. Nevertheless, if the stone has been neither replaced nor re-cut, it does seem remarkable that the lettering should be in such fine condition after 400 years, especially as we know that the other stones had become so degraded as to need re-cutting. For comparison, when in the 1790s James Davenport copied the inscription on Thomas Nash's stone, he found about half of the epitaph illegible and others had complained that visitors examining Shakespeare's bust on the chancel wall were in the process being allowed to walk all over the maledictory gravestone.

*The Tomb of Shakespeare, 1848.*

So, on the one hand we have a denial by the parish clerk that the Shakespeare stone was replaced in the 1830s or '40s, or even re-cut, and on the other a statement by Halliwell that it was replaced, albeit he was confused over when this had happened. Put like that, the odds are against Halliwell; on the other hand, the lettering does seem in very good condition, especially when set against the fact that the adjoining Shakespeare family ledger stones were in such a poor state that they had at least to be recut by the 1840s.

49

*Interior of the Guild Chapel looking east, showing Doom painting above the arch.*

# 5

## The Guild of the Holy Cross and Holy Trinity

### Mairi Macdonald

*Former Head of Local Collections, Shakespeare Birthplace Trust, and Editor of The Register of the Guild of the Holy Cross*

The Bishop of Worcester established a new borough in the parish of Stratford in 1196, although a church had existed on a site by the Avon since Saxon times. In 1269, the new borough had the prospect of a new religious building, within the borough boundaries, when the bishop granted permission to the lay brothers & sisters of the fraternity or Guild of the Holy Cross to build a hospital (or hostel), including a chapel, in the borough. Chaplains would serve in the chapel, praying for the souls of Guild members' ancestors, while the hospital would be for the maintenance of the chaplains, worthy brothers & sisters, and needy priests of the diocese. To support these aims the Guild was allowed to acquire property and income. The chapel was not intended at this date to be for the use of the general lay membership, although they quickly came to dominate the organization. As early as 1292, members were paying 'light money' for candles, which were to burn before the guild's altar, not in the Guild Chapel but in Holy Trinity Church.

There are also references to a fraternity of the Blessed Virgin Mary, or at least a dedicated altar and priest, to which grants of land were made. In 1308, this fraternity had its own officials, but devotion centred on an elaborate Lady Chapel in Holy Trinity. This was clearly of importance: indulgences were granted in 1313 and 1314 to those contributing to the erection or repair of the fabric and in 1367 to those visiting and saying 'Ave' five times.

*Bishop Godfrey Giffard, who in 1269 granted a licence to Robert de Stratford to establish the Guild of the Holy Cross and to build a chapel for the use of the Brethren.*

In 1324, a grant was made to the brethren of the Guild of St John the Baptist, implying the existence of a third guild. However, a grant made in 1325 to the fraternity of the Guild of St Mary & St John suggests that this was probably a single organisation with a double dedication. Of these two, or possibly three, guilds, only the Guild of the Holy Cross sent in a return to Richard II's 1389 survey. It is clear that Holy Trinity Church played an important role in the life of the Guild members. For example, quarterly membership fees were paid for a candle lit before the cross in the church at every mass 'so that God and the blessed Virgin and the much to be reverenced Cross may keep and guard all the bretheren and sisteren of the guild from every ill'. When a member of the Guild died, this candle plus eight smaller candles were to be taken from the church to the house of the deceased member, and a percentage of the members were to keep watch and accompany the corpse to church. The Chapel itself was still, however, reserved solely for the clergy.

Through the late 14th century, Guild accounts record regular payments for work in the church, which was being substantially enlarged during this time. For example:

1353-4   A carpenter was paid for working in the church and silk cloth was provided for an altar

1394-5   Work was undertaken on church windows

1397-8   Lead was purchased for the church

This activity continued into the 15th century after the re-foundation by Henry IV in 1403 of a united Guild of the Holy Cross, the Blessed Virgin Mary and St John the Baptist. From this time onwards, the historical documentation becomes more complete. It is clear from the records that the Guild continued to have a strong presence in Holy Trinity Church, even as it grew in wealth and importance. The Guild Chapel was where the chaplains, appointed by the Guild, said divine service for the members, but Holy Trinity Church was

*The seal of the Guild of the Holy Cross, incorporating to left and right of the cross the figures of the Virgin and St John Baptist, referring to the dedications of the two previously separate guilds.*

where the lay body focused its devotion, paying for lights and hanging lamps every year, and for vestments, altar cloths, lecterns and other church furniture throughout the century.

At some time between 1411 and 1417, the dates of a single cumulative account, the Guild paid £9 0s 8d for work painting (or possibly, repainting) the images at the altars of the Holy Cross, the Virgin and St John, and for painting the loft of the Holy Cross altar. David Odgers indicates in another chapter of this book that, even today, fragments of original mediaeval and 16th century colour remain visible, but it is hard to imagine just how bright the church must have been in the 15th century. The Guild bought red lead, white lead, oil, vermilion, indigo, 'Browne of Spayne', green dye, gold and gilt. These were probably for repainting of images, but the painter was also given 2s 6d for '4 Judases newly made'. The total paid to the painter for his work was 32s 2d – a very large sum.

In addition the Guild bought 7 ells of linen for a cloth to hang before the Holy Cross altar. In the same accounts, the £2 10s paid for 'Costs of the Lady Chapel' includes 3 crests and 5s to John Kyrton for making 3 *gargoles* (gargoyles). In 1415 Kyrton & his wife had their entry fine (admission fee) into the Guild remitted in consideration of his work in the Lady Chapel, while Thomas Barbour's and his wife's fees were remitted in return for his making lights (candles or candelabra) of the Guild before the Holy Cross and Mary altars for 10 years. In 1468-9 14 laten bowls were purchased for placing before the cross in the Church; 2s 6d was paid for a 'blodie curteyn' for the altar of the Holy Cross; 12d for buckram to cover the said altar; and 15d for an altar cloth of Holland (fine linen).

Although we know where the Lady Chapel was (the site is now the Clopton Chapel at the east end of the north aisle), it is harder to be definite

*The Clopton Chapel at the east end of the north aisle of the nave in Holy Trinity, formerly the site of the Lady Chapel. The altar to Mary is believed to have been on the east wall, where the monument to the Earl of Totnes now stands.*

as to where the altars dedicated to St John and the Holy Cross were situated. They may have been on the east wall of the north transept, or possibly even in the north aisle, since late 15th century accounts refer to the altar of St John the Baptist beside the Chapel of the Blessed Virgin Mary in the church. Harvey Bloom, in his *Shakespeare's Church*, places all three altars in this area, those of the Cross and St John being situated along the north wall of the aisle. It is also possible that, as in some larger and collegiate churches, there was a second major altar west of the high altar, which was more especially the altar of the laity and usually styled the altar of the Holy Cross, or of the Holy Rood. There may have been a similar arrangement in Holy Trinity Church below the rood loft.

This all seems very straightforward, but, just as the chantry and the associated College of priests grew in prominence during the later 14th century, during the 1420s the Guild itself became increasingly important both financially and socially. Land was acquired and membership grew, and, after the Guild began major building works on a new chancel to the old chapel, some lay devotion seems to have transferred to this re-developed chapel. 1424 sees the first specific reference in the accounts to the 'altar in the chapel' and from this date those altars are usually so designated, although not always clearly. 1428 saw the consecration of the new chapel and there are references to two altars in it.

This increasing prominence of the Guild led to tensions with the Warden of the Collegiate Church and chantry of St Thomas, established in 1331 in the south aisle, which had become a major place of devotion, as other chapters in this book spell out. It is important to remember, too, that both organisations were property owners and the landlords of many parishioners, and both had a financial interest in where offerings, property and legacies were left. These tensions came to a head in 1428 when Richard Praty, Warden of the College, petitioned the Lords of the Council concerning an assault made on the Archbishop of Canterbury's proctor, who was in Stratford to support the Warden's action against various

Behold, brethren how good to dwell and how together pleasant in unity it is for

Robert de Stratford In 1269 was appointed first Master of the Guild by Giffard, Bishop of Worcester

*Robert de Stratford, who in 1269 was appointed first Master of the Guild by Giffard, Bishop of Worcester. Stained glass by Vernon Spreadbury, installed in 1970.*

people for actions against the liberty of the Church and the rights of the College. A group of nine townspeople, including six prominent members of the Guild, led a crowd who chased the proctor into a house, where 'only the intervention of God' prevented him being burned to death. The Warden described these events as *'orible'* and *'eynnus ryot'* and the townsmen as *'come rebelles'*. Sadly we don't know exactly what the offences against the liberty of the Church and the rights of the College were, but I cannot believe the offences were motivated by purely ecclesiastical differences.

The tensions may have been heightened by the earlier confirmation to the Guild, by Pope Eugenius IV, of the right to have mass and other divine services celebrated, in the chapel, by the Guild's own and other fit priests 'saving the right of the parish church'. This provided another opportunity for those who did not wish to walk as far as the parish church to hear mass, make confession and so forth. The issue was resolved by the pronouncement of ordinances by Thomas, Bishop of Worcester, in 1429, which established the ecclesiastical superiority of the parish church and college over the Guild chaplains. The ordinances provided that once a year, on the wake (patronal festival) of Holy Trinity Church, all offices should cease in the Guild Chapel and all chaplains and clerks should assist at services in the parish church, and make their oblations (offerings) at principal mass 'in order to show themselves to be parishioners of the said church'. All Guild members were to attend both mass & vespers and 4s per annum was to be paid to the church on the day of dedication. The major causes of dispute can be gathered from the prohibitions. These laid down that on Sundays and greater feasts, when a dead body is present or an anniversary celebrated in Holy Trinity Church,

*The Guild Chapel viewed from the north along Chapel Street,*
*with the Guildhall and Almshouses beyond in Church Street.*

the chaplains will not begin mass in the Guild Chapel until the Gospel has been read at High Mass in the church, unless the malice of the Warden wilfully delays this to prevent the Guild Chaplains observing the prohibition. The Chaplains, moreover, were to swear not to stir up strife but to do their best to make peace between the Warden and his parishioners; they were not to entice the parishioners from hearing divine service in Holy Trinity Church; were to do nothing to prejudice the honour of Holy Trinity or its Warden; and they were not to hear confessions of

*Interior of the Guild Chapel looking towards the west and the newly-installed organ.*
*The remains of the wall painting of the martyrdom of St Thomas are to the left.*

the Warden's parishioners without his licence, unless they had a licence from the Warden's superiors (this would allow the Chaplains to serve the spiritual needs of extra-parochial Guild members).

Financial concerns had clearly exacerbated the underlying tussle over spiritual supremacy. The Chaplains, we learn, were to swear to hand over to the Warden all the oblations (charitable offerings) made in the chapel or oratory, and were to swear not to administer any sacrament or sacramental (religious or ritual action) to the Warden's parishioners without his licence, nor to celebrate or receive trentals (payments for requiem masses) to his prejudice. Interestingly, the papal confirmation of these ordinances was obtained in 1432 at the petition of the Master of the Hospital of the Holy Cross, Stratford, and the accounts for that year record payments to Master Thomas Hanwell 'when he went to Rome for our bull' (papal pronouncement). Thereafter the Guild accounts record the annual payment of 4s on the day of dedication of the church; and payments to the altars in the church for wax, vestments and other necessaries continue as before, with additional references to the High Cross in the Chapel of the Guild and the altar there. Regularly, 80lbs of wax was purchased for candles, and oil for hanging lamps, so clearly the church would have been a much darker place without the Guild's especial care of their 3 altars.

A 1442 charter of Henry VI decreed that Guild priests in their copes and gowns were to attend the church at four principal feasts and perform divine service in the choir, staying there until mass was finished, 'saving that one pryste abydyth at home to do dyvyne servyce to the pore pepull and impotent' (infirm). In 1453, the Guild paid for a breakfast in the Guildhall on the feast of the dedication of the church 'for the profit of' the Guild. One of the Guild Chaplains, John Kynges, even left a legacy in 1486 to the altars of the Virgin, St John and Holy Trinity (sic) in the church. Wardens and Sub-wardens of the College, who had previously only rarely been invited, now regularly became members of the Guild, including Thomas Balsale, Warden of the College from 1466, whose tomb survives in the chancel (see pages 21-22), and who was admitted to the Guild while Sub-warden of the College of St Martin, Oxford, in 1455. He was almost certainly a close relation, if not the son, of the Thomas Balsale who served as Master of the Guild in 1454-56 and 1462-63.

*'Big School' with eighteenth-century desks and master's chair
at the north end of the upper level of the fifteenth-century Guildhall.*

In 1482, when a detailed agreement was drawn up between the Guild and its new schoolmaster, a period of six months' notice on either side was provided for, subject to the oversight and advice of the Bishop of Worcester and the Warden of the College. A more tangible sign of the friendly relations between the two organisations, Guild and College, may be seen in the fragmentary wall painting in the Guild Chapel depicting the martyrdom of Thomas Becket (see p.86), to whom the chantry in Holy Trinity Church was dedicated. These paintings date from around 1500 when the nave of the chapel was rebuilt under a scheme initiated and paid for by Hugh Clopton, mercer and Lord Mayor of London, and probably reflect the fact that both bodies had reached an amicable *modus vivendi* after the tensions of the 1420s.

It seems clear that, despite the building of their own chapel, with priests to pray for them and to say mass or hear confession, most members of the Guild still paid devotion to their earlier altars in Holy Trinity Church and perhaps, as membership declined in the years before the Reformation, the role of the chapel reverted to supporting those too aged or infirm to get to Holy Trinity itself.

An inventory of Guild goods in 1475 lists, *inter alia*, 60 items associated with the 3 altars in Holy Trinity, including: 2 copes of red & green with lions of gold; a red cope with gold birds; a green cope with swans; a green & blue cope with lilies in pots; 8 sets of vestments; a pall branched with roses and flowers; together with 10 altar cloths, frontals and other decorative items, most of them embroidered and painted cloths. There were also painted cloths to be used at various seasons, among them one 'of our lady wt thre maryes, a noder of the coronacion of our lady', and 'a steyned clothe of Seynte Gregory'. Particularly intriguing is the reference to an unlikely 'brusshe of pekokes fedurs'.

Given the amount of light at their altars, and their images and vestments, there can be no doubt that, in addition to a devotional presence, the Guild had a strong and vibrant physical presence in Holy Trinity Church throughout the Guild's history. This is a presence which, like Thomas Becket's Chapel, has been largely forgotten by parishioners and visitors alike, in view of the enduring focus on the Cloptons and, of course, on William Shakespeare.

*The thirteenth century lancet windows in the South Transept of the Church.*

# 6

## The South Transept and South Aisle

### Robert Bearman

*Former Head of Archives and Local Studies, Shakespeare Birthplace Trust and author of studies of Stratford buildings and local history*

The north and south transepts are the earliest parts of the church easily visible today. There was an important earlier minster church here, and parts may be buried in the existing fabric, but until about 1200 Stratford was just a village with a handful of houses around the church. Then, in that year, the lord of the manor, who also happened to be the diocesan bishop, the Bishop of Worcester, laid out a new town to the north on the present grid of streets which within fifty years had become a flourishing urban development. This led to a more or less complete rebuilding of the church in around 1250, comprising a central tower, with a steeply-pitched nave, chancel and transepts radiating out from it. The nave and chancel have gone but we still have the transepts, now sandwiched between later nave aisles on the west and an even later chancel on the east.

So how do we know the transepts are 13th century? The main clue is in the windows, tall lancets typical of that date. There are two of these in the east wall of the south transept and there were once two in the west wall although one was blocked when the south aisle was built (or rebuilt): it was only when workmen were knocking a hole through the transept wall in the 1890s to install a new organ that it reappeared (see below). There was talk of saving it, but there had been such a long drawn-out controversy about repositioning the organ that no-one could face yet another hold-up, and so it was demolished. The north transept also had one of its windows blocked up when the north aisle was rebuilt but you can at least still the see its original hood mould.

These early transepts originally had arches leading out through their east and west walls into, we think, earlier aisles. This is no longer obvious in the south transept, but in the north transept there are remains of both of these arches with capitals of mid-13th century date. There were similar features in the south transept, described by the local antiquarian, John Jordan, writing in the 1780s. He begins by describing the south aisle, and the altar of St Thomas at its east end before beginning a new page. The top of this page is

*13th century capital of the blocked arch leading from north transept to chancel aisle.*

damaged, so we can't be absolutely sure what he is saying, but it seems to read:

> From behind the a[?ltar of St Thomas there is] a passage through a very plain Norman Gothic [arch ......... ?] (since filled up with the tomb of Richard Hill) into the South transept of the Cross aisle.

Later, when discussing the east wall of the transept, he adds that when they were making an entrance into a new vestry room 'there was a Gothic arch discovered, exactly correspondent with that above mentioned on the west side'. This vestry is shown on one of Jordan's drawings and its existence is confirmed by another antiquarian, R.B. Wheler, who refers to it as a small vestry, or sacristy, built in 1773, accessed by a doorway cut through the east wall of the transept: 'a small brick room, ill corresponding with any other part of the church'. It was demolished in the 1830s restoration, but traces of a building in this position can still be seen on the exterior south wall of the chancel. So there were indeed arches in the south transept leading out into narrow aisles of some sort, just as they did in the north, with those on the west blocked up when the aisles were rebuilt in the 14th century.

Today's steeply-pitched roofs of both transepts also suggest a 13th-century date, but only as the result of later restoration. Around 1500, there was talk of rebuilding the transepts, or 'cross aisle' as the feature was called. In his will of 1496, Hugh Clopton left £50 'to the new making of the Crosse Ile ... to be paide by myne executours as the works goeth fourth', a phrase echoed by Thomas Hannys in 1503, who gave £6 13s 4d 'towarde the new bielding of the crosse yles within the parrishe churche of Stratford upon Aven ... as the workes goo forward'. So what actually happened?

*John Jordan's late 18th-century drawing of the south elevation of Holy Trinity Church, showing the south transept after the removal of its steeply-pitched 13th-century roof.*

65

The lancet windows establish that the transepts weren't completely rebuilt but, as we can see from early views, both clearly had their original steeply-pitched roofs removed to be replaced by shallower pitched ones, helpfully leaving the original weather moulds so that we can still see exactly where they were. This development also had an effect on both north and south windows. Like today, they are shown with five lights but, unlike today, with flattened heads, and looking much more like c.1500, or later, in date. The observant John Jordan, writing in the 1780s, describes these features:

> ...by the flashings on each side the Tower still visible, it is plainly to be observed that the original roof terminated in a gable or pointed ridge, which was taken down and reduced to a platform surmounted with a parapet wall, as it now remains. It may also be farther observed that the windows at each end have undergone considerable alterations ... From their present appearance it may be conjectured they have been reduced one fourth of their original height and altered from a pointed arch into that of a elipsis to make them correspond with the present roof.

Jordan goes on to say that 'the Structure was ... new cased, as is now discernible in the outward wall and Buttress'. Early views of both transepts do indeed show that the east windows were blocked off and in R.B. Wheler's drawing of the north transept, the whole structure does appear to have been encased in some way.

However, Jordan did not think that these alterations were linked to the Clopton and Hannys bequests of c.1500, mainly because of another piece of evidence available to him which has since disappeared, namely a plaque once above the south window in the south transept, bearing the date 1589 and the initials NT and RH. Jordan suggested these were the initials of the churchwardens of the day, and this has proved to be the case, namely Nicholas Tibbits and Richard Hornby. He suggested that the plaque was put there in 1589 to record changes which took place at that time. In support of this idea, accounts have since come to light to confirm that the parishioners were indeed engaged in repair work at around the relevant date. Before the Reformation, overall maintenance of the church was the responsibility of the College but thereafter became the shared responsibility of the Corporation and the Churchwardens although they were forever arguing as to who should do what. In 1595, we now know the churchwardens accounted for £104 6s 11d spent the previous year 'upon the repaier of the Chancell & an Isle called St Thomas Isle' (i.e. the south aisle), including work on the 'roofs', 'casting and laying the lead' and for glazing, for which they were appealing to the Chancellor of the Exchequer for relief. Emergency work, then, was in hand in connection with the south aisle ('St Thomas Isle') and the chancel in the mid-1590s, giving some support to the idea that the patching up of the transepts, including re-roofing and the alterations to the north and south transept windows, were an earlier phase of the work.

*The south aisle looking towards the Becket Chapel and organ case.*

With regard to the south aisle, its construction was part of a grand rebuilding of the nave and aisles in the first half of the fourteenth century. Various 'indulgences' survive to indicate building work in the north aisle in 1312-13 (the Lady Chapel), at the base of the tower in 1325 and in the south aisle by 1331. This is where John de Stratford, then bishop of Winchester, founded his chantry attached to the altar of St Thomas the martyr, to be served by five other chaplains to celebrate divine service daily. Within a few years the chantry had been endowed with a significant amount of property including, within five years, the advowson of the church itself and its associated revenues, mainly in the form of tithes. Within twenty years a College had been built on nearby land to house the priests, more or less on the site of today's Methodist church.

Little of the chantry's former glory is still reflected in the current fabric (see p.80). Again we have John Jordan to thank for the earliest description of what the chapel was like:

> There is an avenue between the two rows of pews at the east end of the nave that leads to the south [cross-] aisle, a very uniform and regular structure divided into six compartments and strengthened on the outside by buttresses finished with foliage and mitres. .. At the east end was the chapel of St Thomas the martyr founded and rebuilt as was the whole aisle by John Stratford first bishop of Winchester in the reign of King Edward the iid and archbishop of Canterbury Lord chancellor and lord Treasurer to king Edward the third.... Here was an altar, the ascent [i.e. step up] to which is now remaining, and in the south wall are three niches canopied crowned and ornamented with carved work. In each niche is a stone seat which it is presumed were for officiating priests of this chantry to rest themselves during the intervals of divine service while the choir sang their devotional anthems either to the praise of St Thomas or the glory of god.

Also, in Jordan's day, though he doesn't mention it, much of the south aisle (and the north one) was taken up by galleries, built in 1754.

Illustrations are difficult to find but one at least shows their basic form in the north aisle and it is probable they would have been basically the same in the south. Early views also make clear that, following the Reformation, the nave became the only functioning part of the church, converted into what was effectively a preaching area, with altars and chapels a thing of the past, and the chancel and transepts boarded off and allowed to fall into virtual disuse until the Victorians came to their rescue.

Returning to the transept, various accounts survive of the monuments found there, including William Thomas's description, in his expanded edition of William Dugdale's *Antiquities of Warwickshire*, published in 1730, of Richard Hill's famous tomb of 1593 against the west wall, with its inscription in four languages. R.B. Wheler, in 1806, describes it as 'within an arch, in the west wall, at the south end of the transept', indicating that it had always been there, though whether the arch was cut to take it or was already there is difficult to say. In the

*Richard Hill tomb monument in south transept.*

1890s it suffered in the restoration, when the arch was rather too severely remodelled to the extent of obscuring some of the words. Various other listings of the eighteenth-century monuments survive, one the work of William Paine (to Edward Gibbs, 1788) and three by Stratford craftsman, Edward Grubb, including one to Edward Hiccox, who died in 1784.

In the late 1830s, the church was restored under the supervision of Harvey Eginton of Worcester (see p.12). There are some drawings and detailed specifications for parts at least of the restoration, with an emphasis on the laying of a new floor in the nave and providing new pews and galleries. A number of photographs show the effect of this, particularly in the nave but also, obliquely, in the south aisle, replete with their new galleries, with two memorials just visible against the east wall of the aisle.

*South transept, after alterations in the 1830s, to restore it to its original proportions.*

As far as the transepts are concerned, the brick-built vestry shown on Jordan's drawing was demolished, but otherwise the specifications are not very informative. Instructions to the carpenter suggest that the floor was simply boarded over and the mason was required to open up the lancet windows, part of the process of stripping off the plaster or stucco which, according to Jordan's account, and as shown in early drawings, encased both north and south transepts. This must also have been the time when the steeply pitched roofs were reinstated in both transepts and the gable of the north and south walls rebuilt to carry them, together with the reconstruction of the north and south windows to their present form. The change in stonework is still clearly visible.

Another 'improvement', much criticised at a later date by James Halliwell, was the replacement in 1840 of the *sedilia* in the Becket Chapel with reproductions (see p.91). The originals were in a bad state but Halliwell describes them as 'ruthlessly discarded'. He continues:

> A number of those remains coming into my possession about the year 1860, I gave them in behalf of the church to the vicar, and they are, I believe, still to be seen in the churchyard. Whether it would be desirable or even practicable to restore them to their ancient position I am not competent to say but the subject is at all events one that deserves investigation.

*View of nave in painting c.1860, showing galleries in the north and south aisles. Note the absence of the organ case over the arch.*

71

From the mid-1880s there had been growing pressure for further restoration of the church, and one of the first tasks undertaken was the removal of the galleries and pews from the nave installed only fifty years earlier. Photographs survive to establish that for a year or two in the mid-1880s views down the nave and south aisle were less cluttered, with glimpses in the south aisle of the reconstructed *sedilia* of the 1840s and the monuments still *in situ* against the east wall.

This situation did not last long. As early as March 1873, there had been complaints that the organ, then sited in the north transept, should be moved as 'half the power of the organ is lost by the pillars of the tower'. But it was not until 1888-9 that its removal was at last effected. The scheme, first outlined in October 1888, involved splitting the organ, placing the 'great organ and a small part of the pedal organ' over the central tower arch in the nave, with the 'choir, swell and remaining portion of the pedal organ' installed at the east end of the south aisle. To make room for the second part of the

*Drawing of south transept in 1880s, before installation of the organ.*

scheme, it was at first proposed to cut an opening 13 feet wide and 19 feet high in the dividing wall between aisle and transept. The architect took exception to this and so it was agreed instead to fit the whole of this section of the organ into the south aisle, behind a wooden oak screen designed by Messrs Bodley and Garner and executed by Mr Franklin of Deddington, Oxford. This meant the effective obliteration of the heart of the old Becket chapel as well as the taking down of the monument to Sir Reginald Forster, who had died in 1705, and his wife, Mary daughter of Edward Nash (d. 1731), and re-siting it in the north transept where it can still be seen.

It was during this effective dismemberment of the St Thomas Chapel that workmen found buried in the floor what was believed to be the medieval altar slab, or *mensa*, in Purbeck marble, the use of which had in effect been banned at the Reformation three centuries earlier. Whether it was deliberately hidden there, in the hope that it could be retrieved in the event of an early Catholic revival depends on one's view of how enthusiastically the new forms of worship were adopted. But looking at it from a more practical point of view, altars had been dismantled under Edward VI, reassembled under Mary, and then dismantled again under Elizabeth. Perhaps the cost-conscious churchwardens simply had an eye to further expense when, second-time round, they decided to make it part of the floor in case it was needed again. On its eventual unearthing, it was placed on the high altar in 1892 (see p.96).

The compromise arrangement over the organ ushered in a long-running dispute between the Restoration Committee and the organ builders, who complained that it was impossible to bring the old instrument, albeit reconstructed, back to a high standard, especially within the cramped space available. This rumbled on for years but nothing much happened until the late 1890s when, with the restoration of the chancel at an end, attention turned to the nave and transepts. It was hoped that one way of raising the necessary funds would be to repeat the highly successful campaign of the 1870s and 1880s, by which Americans had been encouraged to donate money for the introduction of stained glass into one of the chancel windows. This time, the money raised was used for stained glass in the south window of the south transept, designed by Messrs

Heaton and Butler. It was unveiled, somewhat precipitately, by the American ambassador in 1896, before the money had been raised, and it was not until early in the next century that the debt was paid off, mainly owing to the generosity of the novelist Marie Corelli.

By early 1898 the complete restoration of the nave, aisles and transepts had been completed, pushed through by the vicar, the indefatigable George Arbuthnot. In general terms this involved pulling up the floors laid in the 1830s which were found to conceal the many ledger stones of earlier floors. These were also taken up, exposing in turn several vaults, particularly in the

*Original 13th century window in the west wall of the south transept, discovered during alterations in 1898.*

south aisle. The installation of a new under-floor heating system broke into others, though readers of the *Parish Magazine* and the *Stratford Herald* were reassured that any bones disturbed were respectfully re-interred. Some of the ledger stones were re-laid in the aisles and transepts but not in their original positions. Others were simply lost following the decision to lay wooden blocks over the areas to be used for seating.

In the south transept, the plan adopted was the creation of a central stone aisle running north-south, made up in part of displaced ledger stones, flanked by wooden flooring for the seating. Only four of the stones recorded by Jordan in the late 18th century as lying in the south transept are still to be found there. Seven were re-laid in the south aisle and five in the north aisle, while two seem to be lost.

In early 1898, a significant discovery was made, to which reference has already been made. One feature of the restoration was to be the building of a new organ. To get round the problems which had been caused by the relocation of the old organ in the south aisle, it was at last agreed that the west wall of the transept should be pierced with an arch, 10 feet by 12 feet, to accommodate the proposed new organ. During the work, the remains of the original 13th-century south-west transept window were uncovered directly over the Hill tomb. There was a lively debate over whether it should be preserved. The vicar and the architect were initially all for retaining it but backed down in face of the determination of the Committee to get the work done. This was when much work to the surrounds of the Hill tomb was carried out and also a number of wall monuments taken down and repositioned. The 'engine and feeders of the organ' were located at the south end of the transept behind a screen, in front of which was placed the altar. The space behind the screen may also have served as a small vestry as, in 1909, there is reference to the screen being brought forward by about 4 feet to create a larger vestry.

Further changes were made immediately after the First World War, the effect of which was to turn the south transept, officially renamed St Peter's chapel, into a memorial chapel for those killed in the War. The proposal was first made in March 1917 but the chapel was not dedicated until April 1920. The principal additions were the oak screen dividing the chapel from the crossing, designed by

*Reredos with names of Stratford men who died in the First World War, on altar in the Becket chapel.*

Guy Pemberton and made by Messrs Haughton of Worcester. A reredos was added to the altar, adapted from a shrine given in memory of Robert Noakes, also designed by Guy Pemberton, on which were inscribed the names of other Stratford men who had died. This fine piece of work has since been moved to the altar in the south aisle.

Additions in similar vein were made in the 1920s. In 1925 a proposal was made for a memorial tablet to actors who had died in the War. It was designed by leading sculptor, George Frampton (1860-1928), and was originally intended for the chancel. But there were difficulties in obtaining a faculty and it was therefore placed in St Peter's Chapel instead, unveiled by the actor and theatre manager, Sir Johnston Forbes-Robertson in 1925. It is still there though not perhaps displayed to its best advantage. This was followed in 1929 by a memorial to the 61st (South Midland) Division

*St Peter's Chapel as it was in 2013, before the latest restoration, seen through the opening in the screen that connects the Chapel with the Crossing.*

in memory of the officers and men who had fallen in the First World War. Designed by Captain R.B. Saunders, winner of the Military Cross, it was placed in a medieval altar recess in the east wall, its present position. This recess would have served as a pre-Reformation altar for a chapel, originally no doubt with *piscina* (stone basin) alongside, although we know little about it. There was a matching one in the north transept, which does have the remains of a *piscina*, thought to have been dedicated to St Katherine, and several medieval wills contain minor bequests to it.

Further changes later in the century, particularly in 1976, were designed to improve the clergy vestry by further rearrangement of the screen which had once stood against the south wall but in 2016 the building of a new vestry along the external wall of the south aisle, provided the opportunity to return the screen to its original position, creating a space much as it had looked when built in the thirteenth century (see p.18).

A puzzling feature is a mutilated monument, on the east wall of the south transept, to Henry Oliver Hunt (died 1874) and his sister Harriet Hunt (died 1865). Clearly it was not there in 1929 when a photograph of the chapel was taken, but nor was it listed amongst the monuments in the church recorded by Bloom in his *Shakespeare's Church*, published in 1902. Hunt took his own life in 1874 'whilst of unsound mind' but why his monument, wherever it had originally been placed, was moved to this position some time after 1929 has yet to be explained.

Finally some brief discussion of the Thomas a Becket chapel once in the south aisle, to supplement the information in Ronnie Mulryne's chapter in this book. Its heart was the east bay of the south aisle currently occupied by the organ. It must have been enclosed by a screen though no-one is quite sure how far west it extended. Some argue for two further bays, based on the fact that the button decoration on the ceiling is restricted to that area, but this is far from certain. The altar would have been against the east wall, no doubt with a *piscina*, and in Jordan's day there was still a step up to it. The three seats, the *sedilia*, though rebuilt in 1840, are in their original position, testifying to the altar's importance. Jordan also refers to an archway forming an opening from the aisle to the transept.

St Thomas's chapel was the most important of the seven or eight which existed in pre-Reformation times, or at least of altars in saints' names. Some, linked to the guilds were in the north aisle, and two others in the transepts have already been mentioned. But it was the St Thomas chapel, served by the body of priests, which in the 1330s evolved into the collegiate establishment responsible for running the church until the Reformation. Evidence about its activities is not as abundant as that for the Stratford guilds, but we do know, from the will of William Bell, who died in 1465, that there were statues in the chapel of St Dominic and Our Lady of Pity before whom lights were to be burnt, and a crop of six other testators left money to the altar between 1500 and 1543. When a

*Oblique view from choir stalls of the organ console and the wooden oak screen designed by Messrs Bodley and Garner to conceal the organ.*

petition was filed in 1336 for financial support, the chantry was described as 'seemly & decent ... beautiful to any beholder', where divine worship was performed, though this could be done more effectively, it was argued, if means could be found to increase the number of priests. The chapel was said to be busy all day, with people from both Stratford and elsewhere. Indeed it was claimed that the town's population was 3,000, almost certainly an exaggeration, many of whom came to the chantry 'on account of its suitability and their devotion to it'. By way of contrast, buildings for the priests were inadequate 'ruinous and the greater part of them fallen to the ground' whilst the warden had no plot of land suitable for erection of sufficient houses for them. The chapel had an income of sorts, but without further support it was feared that the warden and priests would be forced to beg 'to the disgrace of their order'. As it was, they were overburdened with expense because of the crush of visitors to the chantry and the heavier burdens laid on them through 'worldly malice and the passage of time'. All this had the desired effect and the chantry was subsequently richly endowed and re-organised into a collegiate organisation which throve for a couple of hundred years.

The south transept and south aisle have therefore been focal points of worship within the church for centuries and this continues today, although the historical significance of these parts of the church may not be immediately apparent to the casual visitor.

*The Becket Chapel as it is today, following conservation.*

# 7

## The Thomas Becket Chapel: Its history and people

### Ronnie Mulryne

*Chairman of the Friends of Shakespeare's Church*

The Thomas Becket chapel at the east end of Holy Trinity's south aisle – today a rather undistinguished-looking part of the church – could be said to reflect not only the early history of Holy Trinity, but more widely the early history of the English church as a whole. At a stretch, it might be argued that it reflects the history of England struggling in the pre-Reformation period to reconcile religion with politics. This is altogether too broad a canvas for a single chapter. Yet, as one speaker in the 'Taste of History' series suggested, the Becket chapel and its altar would be seen as the primary source of Holy Trinity's fame, were it not for overwhelming public interest in the Church's Shakespeare connections. The Becket chapel remains for many parishioners a sacred space for prayer and devotion, but few would claim that the remarkable tale for which it stands is widely known.

### The Thomas Becket story

Thomas Becket's life-story reaches us over a gap of 850 years. Remarkably, given this distance in time, most people have heard of Becket's name and his repute as churchman and martyr. He was born on 21 December 1120, and assassinated in his cathedral at Canterbury on 29 December 1170. Becket had a meteoric career in public service as Royal Chancellor and confidant to kings, before his iconic appointment as Archbishop of Canterbury in 1162. With astonishing, perhaps unprecedented, haste Becket was canonised (recognised as a saint) on Ash Wednesday 1173, within three years of his assassination. This followed a process of deliberation which a cautious Church routinely extended to

*Martyrdom of St Thomas of Canterbury, in a woodcut in 'The Golden Legend'.*

many decades. Such relative haste was due, no doubt, to the high profile of the murdered Archbishop, to the notoriety of the murder, and to the place and Christmas season in which it was committed. It reflects too a fundamental principle which the Church, many worshippers, and pre-eminently Becket himself, believed the assassination violated: the right of the Church to be free from interference by the secular authorities in Church business, including the rules of conduct for individuals.

It is true that the Church's freedom was understood at the time to include a right to the acquisition of property and the ownership of exceptional wealth, together with a right to set up courts, hold trials and impose penalties across a defined range of offences. 'Freedom' also implied rights to a status that conflicted with the status enjoyed by the king, not only in ceremonial matters but also in those deeper questions of public allegiance on which royal authority ultimately depends. Becket was far from being the first or the only cleric to perceive a divided loyalty to church on the one hand and state on the other. Twenty-five years before Thomas's birth, Saint Anselm of Canterbury had put the matter succinctly in an explosively-phrased question at the Council of Rockingham (1095): "Is the duty I owe to the pope compatible with the obedience I owe to the king?" The well-worn phrase 'render unto Caesar …' might offer a response, but the conflict of loyalties St Anselm identified was not easy to disentangle. Moreover, in Becket's day, and even more acutely in the four or five centuries that followed, divided loyalties became an intensely political matter directly affecting everyday life.

Perhaps Becket's personality made the church-and-politics conflict worse. Described by his most recent biographer, the historian John Guy, as tall, good-looking and clever, and by his contemporary and friend, John of Salisbury, as 'a charmer', Becket nevertheless provoked a long series of

*The assassination of Thomas Becket, wall painting in the Church of St Peter ad Vincula, South Newington. Becket is shown kneeling at his altar, with the chalice and ministering priest also depicted.*

quarrels with his secular overlord King Henry II. It's true that he had mellowed, or so it seems, from impulsive youth and quarrelsome early celebrity to become a subtle politician and devoted priest. Guy describes 'Becket's journey from the worldly warrior-chancellor to the conflicted, brave, otherworldly priest and victim of his later years'. Yet, when it came to the moment at which he faced death, even John of Salisbury, usually admiring, thought the Archbishop could have saved himself by behaving in a more tactful and conciliatory manner. Perhaps the knights who acted as the King's self-chosen agents in the assassination were mistaken when they came to believe that Henry wanted revenge on his Archbishop – it seems he never explicitly said so – and perhaps Becket, true to his ingrained personality, behaved provocatively as the knights intruded into his Cathedral. Yet when he lay dying in agony and cried out 'For the name of Jesus and the protection of the Church I am ready to embrace death', it would be a hard heart that supposed he was anything other than sincere – sincerely committed, that is to say, to his faith. T.S. Eliot makes his play *Murder in the Cathedral* pivot on the questions: 'Was Becket's stance mere arrogance? And, if so, does this invalidate his claim to martyrdom?' Of course, to many minds Becket's dedication to his Church, and his intense capacity for self-giving, rise above the intellectual and theological qualms Eliot so brilliantly raises.

We may have other misgivings about worshipping at an altar dedicated to St Thomas. The immediate response to his murder of Becket's Canterbury contemporaries will strike today's church-goers as distasteful and bizarre, if not downright idolatrous. The martyr's blood and brains were scooped up, placed in a silver basin and kept for use in future reliquaries. Bystanders brought tiny bottles and made off with as much of the spilled blood as they could, to keep or to sell. The martyr's blood was subsequently diluted with water by Church authorities, became known as the water of Canterbury, was sold for profit, and was supposed to have performed many miracles.

## Becket's martyrdom cult

A cult based on the martyrdom grew up immediately, with images of Becket displayed everywhere across Western Christendom. These include illuminated manuscripts from as early as 1180, including a manuscript copy, now in the British Library, of John of Salisbury's eye-witness account of the martyrdom, and a manuscript psalter dating to 1225, also owned by the British Library, with an illustration of the moment when one of the King's knights, sword drawn, strikes the Archbishop on the head.

The production of stained glass followed suit, with magnificent examples still surviving in a twelfth-century window at Chartres Cathedral and, much nearer home, in a restored, originally fifteenth-century, window in the Beauchamp Chapel at St Mary's, Warwick. An early window in Christ Church Cathedral, Oxford, with the head of Becket defaced, probably at the Reformation, shows the knights attacking the kneeling archbishop, swords raised high.

*Enamelled reliquary casket, c.1180-90, made in Limoges, France, depicting the martyrdom of St Thomas (V&A).*

Precious artefacts were created, such as a superb thirteen-century enamelled and gilded chest depicting Becket's martyrdom, now in the Louvre, or the Limoges-enamel Becket casket or 'Chasse' in the Victoria & Albert Museum.

Wall paintings, the plain man's way of learning about the horrific martyrdom, appeared everywhere, with at least two surviving examples close to Holy Trinity: a horribly graphic depiction of the scalping of Becket in the Church of St Peter ad Vincula, South Newington near Banbury, and, nearer still, one of the wall paintings still partially visible in Stratford's Guild Chapel.

*Painting of Becket martyrdom on west wall of the nave in the Guild Chapel c.1500, as depicted by Thomas Fisher in 1804 following rediscovery of the wall paintings.*

It would scarcely be an exaggeration to say that in the mid- to-later Middle Ages Thomas Becket became the most famous man – and saint – in Europe, and the focus of intense devotion according to the religious customs of the age. For today's church-goers, in the uneasy accommodation that persists between politics and faith, the need is to separate the principles for which Becket stood from the man himself, and from the religious practices that once expressed devotion. Are we justified in continuing Sunday by Sunday to honour the twelfth-century saint by worshipping at his altar?

## John de Stratford and the Chantry Chapel of St Thomas

It should be no surprise that when an extraordinarily gifted fourteenth-century son of Stratford became sufficiently prominent, and sufficiently wealthy, to act as a high-profile benefactor of his local church, his benefaction should be dedicated to Thomas Becket. John de Stratford was born into a prosperous burgher family about one hundred years after Becket's murder. His early education is unknown – he may well have been schooled at Holy Trinity under the schoolmaster of the local Guild, possibly one of the clergy attached to the Church. We know that he attended Oxford. He became Rector of Holy Trinity in 1317 and, soon after, a leading counsellor to Edward II. By 1323 he was Bishop of Winchester – King Edward was not consulted by the pope about the appointment, and was furious at such a slight to his royal authority. Despite this, Stratford was appointed Chancellor of England seven years later, an office he held by fits and starts for many years.

In 1331, even though his responsibilities had taken him far from his home town, he founded Holy Trinity's Becket Chapel. In 1333 he became Archbishop of Canterbury and by May 1339 was sufficiently wealthy to serve as guarantor of the king's debts. Despite this illustrious career he quarrelled over the liberties of the Church with both Edward II and his successor Edward III (the so-called 'perfect king'). His was a career and

*John de Stratford, Archbishop of Canterbury, depicted praying in front of the altar in the Becket Chapel. Behind are his brother Robert, Bishop of Chichester, and their kinsman Ralph, Bishop of London. This stained glass window was installed in 1905 in the south aisle of the nave, adjacent to the Becket Chapel.*

a set of moral challenges, that is to say, strongly reminiscent of Thomas Becket's, and one that raised difficult issues for a high royal servant like John de Stratford, just as thoroughly entangled as Becket in questions of allegiance to Church and State.

The foundation of a chantry chapel dedicated to St Thomas was planned initially to support a warden, a sub-warden and three priests, a relatively modest number. Five years later, when John was already three years into the highest preferment of all, the Archbishopric of Canterbury, a formal process increased the number of priests to eleven, a considerable number in comparison to similar foundations elsewhere. This suggests that the aim, at least, was that the chapel should be a rich and active foundation – even though it's by no means certain that all eleven priests ever actually took office.

A chantry chapel's prime function was to offer prayer for the souls of the benefactor and named beneficiaries and for his (sometimes her) family. By the theology of the time, regular prayer in a dedicated chantry would reduce the time spent by a beneficiary in Purgatory, the spiritual state which was a necessary rite of passage for the souls of those who died in the faith. Prayers and gifts offered at the altar would have the further effect of reducing the spiritual debt of those who offered them – thus inviting more praying and more giving – to the enrichment of the altar and the associated church. An early document tells us that the fourteenth-century priests of the Stratford altar were specifically instructed 'to celebrate divine service daily at the altar of St Thomas the Martyr, in the chapel built by the said grantor [John de Stratford] to the south of the said church, for the soul of the said bishop [John again], and for the souls of his father, mother and ancestors'.

*View from north-west of College of Priests, situated close to Holy Trinity.*

The foundation of the Chapel had another and long-lasting outcome. The priests attached to the altar of St Thomas, whether five or eleven in number, were regarded as comprising a 'College' or *collegium* (that is to say a community), leading to Holy Trinity being formally called, then and now, 'The Collegiate Church of the Holy and Undivided Trinity'. Something over 170 churches known as 'collegiate' were founded in England and Wales up to the early years of the 16th century. Most still exist, including the great College of St Mary at Warwick, founded in 1123, which survives today as St Mary's church. In Holy Trinity's case, the chantry priests lived in a college building (see p.89), just west of the church. This came about as the result of the generosity of Ralph de Stratford, another high-flying Stratford Churchman – probably the nephew of John de Stratford – whose career took him from Bishop of London and Dean of the Province of Canterbury to a nomination as Cardinal in 1350. In 1352, four years after the death of John, Ralph provided for a college building for the chantry priests, more or less on the site of today's Methodist Church. This was a substantial stone structure that survived until 1799, when it was demolished.

Chantry chapels varied hugely across the country from imposing royal foundations (for example Henry V's magnificent chantry chapel at Westminster Abbey) to humble structures little more than screens around a grave monument, for example the beautiful restored Chantry chapel at St Peter's Church, Burford, Oxfordshire. On the largest scale, a great stone-built structure, dedicated to Becket, once occupied the centre of old London Bridge. Another bridge chantry, though very considerably more modest, survives where the old bridge in Wakefield meets the bank of the river Calder. More directly comparable to Holy Trinity's Becket chantry is the superb chapel made possible by the wealth of the Beauchamp family at St Mary's Warwick, begun in 1443 and completed in 1452.

The comparison with Warwick tells us little about the actual appearance of Stratford's chantry chapel, since the ambition and scale of the chapel at

St Mary's was, beyond question, considerably greater than even John de Stratford envisaged for Holy Trinity. So far as the detail of the Stratford chapel's appearance is concerned, we have to rely largely on inference. As Robert Bearman reports earlier in this book, we can infer that the Becket chapel must have been enclosed by a screen, no doubt richly carved like other early woodwork in the church. This screen may have been extensive, if we accept that the ceiling bosses surviving in the south aisle mark the chapel's extent, though this remains uncertain. Other features confirm that the chapel must have formed a notable visual and architectural presence in the south aisle, including, as Bearman notes, the three existing (though re-built) *sedilia*, and the step up to the altar described by the antiquarian John Jordan. Given the probable location of the altar itself within the space now occupied by organ pipes, and the very considerable size of the surviving altar stone, mentioned below, we can confidently surmise that the chapel mirrored

*The rebuilt (1840) 'sedilia' or seats for priests serving the Becket altar.*

the wealth devoted to it by its Stratford benefactors. If we can imagine the Church before the present-day pulpit and the organ console were constructed it becomes evident that the Becket chapel and the Becket altar must have formed an imposing presence as a site of worship from the 1330s onward.

When we attempt to reconstruct the early life of the chapel, we again have to rely to some extent on inference, though documentary evidence survives in the Stratford archives, as Mairi Macdonald noted in her report for the Parochial Church Council, commissioned by the Friends of Shakespeare's Church. Here the chapel is described in July 1336, five years after its foundation, as being 'seemly & decent...beautiful to any beholder'. There were initial, if arguably welcome, difficulties. There was insufficient income to sustain the chapel in an appropriate manner, 'there being a large number of people living in the parish who flock daily' to it. Popular success continued as time went on. According to one source, there were more than 3000 people in the parish (a probable exaggeration), 'who come many times to the chantry on account of its suitability and their devotion to it'. Yet this popularity was a mixed blessing. The Warden & priests were said to be overburdened with expenses because of 'the crush of people & the heavier burdens' therefore laid on them. John de Stratford provided funds, as noted above, to increase the number of priests to eleven, so that the financial and personnel difficulties were alleviated, at least in intention. A very unusual step was taken in 1415, after the chantry had been in existence for 80 years or so: the parish Church was appropriated to the chantry, so that the newer foundation in a sense absorbed the earlier – a mark, one assumes, of the chantry's continuing success and importance.

So far as the lives of the priests are concerned, their duties were clearly laid down. Daily mass was to be said for benefactors of the Church, the chapel and the college. On Sundays two priests were required to say mass not only at the Guild's altars but specifically in the Becket chapel. The more domestic side of the priests' lives was also carefully prescribed. Restrictions were imposed on their behaviour: they were to avoid insobriety and drunkenness and were in fact to shun taverns altogether. Nor were the priests to enter any house without the license of the Warden, though the reason for this rule remains tantalisingly unspecified. There were local problems. We hear echoes of tensions between the priests of the college (the chantry priests) and the priests appointed by the Guild of the Holy Cross to serve the Guild's chapels in Holy Trinity. The dispute was only resolved, eventually, when the Bishop of Worcester, the local diocesan, stepped in and specified the rights and privileges of the two religious organisations. In its early years, then, the chantry chapel of St Thomas enjoyed, according to the archives, beauty, popularity as a place of worship, and a high profile, even if such prominence entailed a heavy work-load for the priests, and a measure of local and wider notoriety.

## The Reformation and aftermath

The chapel dedicated to St Thomas, once so prominent and high profile, has disappeared, or almost disappeared, from Holy Trinity. If we ask what happened, the short answer is that the Reformation happened, not only in England, but to differing degrees across Europe. One stimulus to Reform was that the 'burgeoning industry of intercession', as Diarmuid MacCulloch calls it, the main business of chantries and the source of their wealth, had become deeply suspect in the minds of many sincere Christians, not only in response to criticism by theological campaigners such as Martin Luther, but also due to wider cultural change. In England, Henry VIII and his chief minister Thomas Cromwell, motivated in Henry's case by a mix of spiritual conviction, greed and desire for Anne Boleyn, and in Cromwell's by ambition, initiated and carried through a purge of the whole structure of church wealth – thus echoing in high profile the church-and-state conflict of Becket's day and John de Stratford's. Commissioners were sent out across the land, instructed by a document known as the *Valor Ecclesiasticus* (1535). This ordered the commissioners to enquire into all 'cathedral churches, colleges, churches collegiate, houses conventual ... monasteries, priories [and] ... chantries' in England and Wales.

The commissioners came back reporting huge wealth and alleging sexual delinquency among priests and nuns, together with further mis-demeanours both trivial and grave. Henry resolved to expunge this embar-

*Title page of the Great Bible authorised by Henry VIII (1541), who is seen enthroned and dispensing instruction to his clergy and nobility while the common people cry 'May the King live'.*

rassing blot on a church he was convinced needed reform – and to claw back its wealth to the Crown. Achieving this would, in addition, strengthen his personal grip, or would-be grip, on his country's religion, an ambition wonderfully represented by the title page of the Great Bible of 1539-40, where Henry sits dispensing holy writ to his Bishops and great courtiers, while the common people with one voice cry out 'Vivat Rex'.

The smaller monasteries went first, accused of 'manifest sin, vicious, carnal and abominable living'. Next the greater monasteries surrendered 'voluntarily' between 1537 and 1540. When it came to collegiate Churches and chantries, dedication to St Thomas Becket became a special focus of attack. According to G.W. Barnard, Becket was routinely presented as defending 'the detestable and unlawful liberties of the church'. He had been made a saint, it was said, only because he championed the 'usurped authority' of the pope, a form of allegiance deeply displeasing to Henry following his break with Rome. Henry gave orders that Becket should be referred to simply as 'Bishop Becket', not as a saint. He 'ordered that all images and pictures of Becket throughout the realm should be … removed from all churches and chapels, that Becket's feast day should no longer be observed, and that the services in his name should be razed from all service books'.

In 1547, the year in which Henry VIII died and his son Edward VI succeeded to the throne, Stratford's turn came. Both College and Guild were dissolved, the offending wall-paintings in the Guild Chapel, including the panel depicting Becket's martyrdom, were ordered to be whitewashed, and the Becket altar in the chantry chapel was pulled down. Local wealth went, at least initially, to the royal coffers. Perhaps we shouldn't attribute all this destruction solely to orders from royal sources. Local opinion, including notably clerical opinion, may not have been unanimous in upholding the chapel's rights. The bishop of Worcester – the diocesan bishop during the crucial opinion-forming years 1535-1539 – was Hugh Latimer, subsequently famed as a protestant martyr under

Queen Mary. According to the *New Oxford Dictionary of National Biography* Latimer was no friend to chantries, arguing that institutions which 'existed largely to celebrate masses for the dead, including the religious houses and chantries, were redundant, and should be demolished so that their wealth could be redirected ...'. King Henry, never stable in matters of religion, lurched back in the later 1530s towards the old religion – his Six Articles of 1539 virtually endorse the real presence of Christ's Body and Blood in the Mass, a doctrine unthinkable to protestants. The Articles even accepted that masses may benefit the departed soul, a doctrine fundamental to chantries. Latimer spoke against the king in the House of Lords – and was forced to resign his bishopric after four years in office. It was in this alarmingly uncertain religious climate, or its immediate aftermath, that the Reformation brought dissolution to the Stratford Guild and to Stratford's Becket chapel.

*The 'mensa' in position on the high altar, showing pillars to support its width.*

The altar of St Thomas and the enclosing chapel were demolished in, or soon after, 1547, alongside the formal dissolution of the chantry, the college and the Guild. One unpredictable and happy survival, however, remains in Holy Trinity today. In 1889, three-and-a-half centuries after the Chantry was dissolved, the *mensa* or table-top of the original Becket altar was discovered during alterations to the Church's south aisle – 'buried' according to Harvey Bloom, 'beneath the floor'. It was re-located to become the *mensa* of the Church's present High Altar. The surviving altar stone, assuming that its provenance is secure, allows us to make some confirming inferences about the Becket chapel and its altar. The altar must have been splendid, or at least fine, since the *mensa* is of Purbeck marble. It must have been large, since the *mensa* as we have it today measures 9 feet 5 inches by 2 feet 11 inches. We may even be able to grasp something of the original altar's spiritual significance. Three crosses representing the wounds of Christ can still be seen incised into the altar's surface. Another two are now hidden, the reference being to the traditional five wounds suffered by Christ on the Cross. No doubt these devotional symbols would have been regarded as 'popish' when the Commissioners came calling, and perhaps provided another reason, if one were needed, for pulling the altar down.

So ends this strange eventful history. Yet this apparent ending is not of necessity final. The Becket chapel continues to serve the spiritual needs of Holy Trinity's present-day congregation, and we may hope that the Friends of Shakespeare's Church will in the near future find the resources to beautify the chapel's former site. New fabric and new supporting carpentry have been put in place and it is proposed that lighting may be installed to bring out the beauty of the organ case that today forms the chapel's backdrop. Even though shorn of its former glories, this sacred space remains one that incorporates much of the evolving story of Holy Trinity and the remarkable history of its ancient and modern worship.

www.stratford-upon-avon.org

# Index

# Image Credits

## Photographs

| | |
|---|---|
| Robert Bearman | 64, 70 |
| John Cheal | inside front, 14, 15, 16, 20, 21, 22, 23, 27, 28, 29, 30, 32, 33, 34, 45, 62 |
| Jonathan Drake | 25, 26, 50, 57, 58, 67, 75, 76, 80, 91, inside back |
| Richard Lithgow | 83 |
| Harry Lomax | front cover, 6, 17, 18, 36, 37, 38, 39 |
| Lindsay MacDonald | vi, 2, 13, 52, 54, 56, 69, 71, 78, 88 |
| Ronnie Mulryne | 96 |
| William Mulryne | iii, 4 |
| Stephen Oliver | iv, 19 |
| Susan Swann | 60 |
| Shakespeare Birthplace Trust | 35, 53, 65, 74, 94 |
| Victoria & Albert Museum | 85 |

## Illustrations

8   Plan of church drawn by Rodney Melville and Partners, 2013

10   Engraving by Philip E. Massey, *The Building News,* 4 January 1889

12   Engraving by William Butterfield, *The Literary World*, 28 September 1839

40   Drawing by George Vertue, Tour with Lord Oxford, 1737, British Museum

41   Drawing by J.P. Neale, engraved by J. Le Keux, *Views of Collegiate and Parochial Churches in Great Britain,* No. IV, 1824

42   Engraving, *The Illustrated London News*, 18 September 1847

47   Charles J. Langston, *How Shakespeare's Skull was Stolen and Found*, 1884

48   Drawing by Gerald E. Moira, in *Shakespeare's True Life*, James Walter, 1890

49   Drawing by F.W. Fairholt, in *The Home of Shakespeare*, New York, 1848

72   Drawing by Gerald E. Moira, in *Shakespeare's True Life*, James Walter, 1890

82   Woodcut in *The Golden Legend,* by Jacobus de Voragine c.1260, published in English by William Caxton, 1483–84. University of Glasgow

86   Drawing by Thomas Fisher in 1804, published by J.G. Nichols, 1838

89   Drawing by Robert Bell Wheler, engraved by F. Egington, in *History and Antiquities of Stratford-upon-Avon,* 1806